MORE PRAISE FOR *A THOUSAND KISSES*

"John Weiser's book is a sober reminder of the truism that 'while history may not repeat, it does instruct.' ... This book is at once instructive about a family's courage and determination to stay together and the dangers of remaining silent while a government tightens immigration laws and promotes racial scapegoating. This is a heartwarming cautionary tale that speaks to our common humanity and shared responsibilities as citizens."

  — *Stephen A. Privett, S.J., President Emeritus, University of San Francisco*

"This rich account ... will keep the reader glued to a narrative filled with many redemptive moments, often due to the generosity extended by acquaintances and perfect strangers. This account skillfully recreates the palpable tension of multiple escapes that readily engages the reader."

  — *Stephen S. Pearce, Ph.D., Senior Rabbi Emeritus of*
    Congregation Emanu-El of San Francisco

"John Weiser has a most compelling story to tell that is riveting from start to finish. It is really a set of stories: of love between parents, of growing up and coming of age, of a family searching for freedom ..., of coming to America and the realization of a remarkable professional life, ... of the fulfillment, promise, and gratitude of a life fully lived. The writing is exquisite, the character development elegantly depicted, and the stories and challenges engrossing. You will not want to put this book down."

  — *James A. Donahue, Ph.D., President, Saint Mary's College of California*

"... This is a poignant story of hardship, adventure and resilience as a family finds its way out of Europe. ... The author of this memoir has given us an intense and captivating story that reminds us how the experience of just one small family can unfold a universal tale of fear, dislocation, forced migration, and finally triumph while helping others along the way."

  — *Riess Potterveld, President, Graduate Theological Union*

"John Weiser's superbly written memoir is both a beautiful love story (of his father, a renowned doctor, and his mother, a talented musician) and an inspiring refugee story of perseverance, dashed hopes, and resourcefulness. As their ship passed the Statue of Liberty, 9-year-old John summed up their refugee experience, 'I hoped we'd finally find a home.' A unique, inspiring read. Highly recommended."

> — *Joseph Eagan, S.J., author and former professor at the*
> *University of San Francisco*

"John Weiser's excellent memoir is played out against the growth of fascism inEurope and relates the extraordinary efforts of his mother and father to keep the family together and safe in a time of great danger. Exhibiting courage, determination and patience, John's parents led them through not only danger and physical challenges, but also, most frustratingly, through the incredible bureaucratic morass facing those fleeing the Nazi menace. It is a story always worth telling, if only in the hopes that it doesn't happen again."

> —*David E. Collins, former General Counsel and*
> *Vice Chairman of the Board of Johnson & Johnson*

A THOUSAND KISSES

*A Family's Escape from the Nazis
to a New Life*

A THOUSAND KISSES

*A Family's Escape from the Nazis
to a New Life*

John W. Weiser

Project Editor: Sandra Gary

Copy Editor: Sally W. Smith

Book and cover design: Barbara Geisler Design

ISBN-13: 978-1978318076

ISBN-10: 1978318073

Library of Congress Control Number: 2017916236

This book is dedicated first to my wonderful parents.
I wish I had known then all I know now.

It is also dedicated to my children, who had the warm and joyful
experience of knowing my parents, but knew nothing of their history,
since my parents preferred to live in the present; and to my
grandchildren, who did not know their great-grandparents,
but can now know the family's history.

Finally, this book is dedicated to my wife, Maria, whose love and
steady support have been a priceless gift for over 60 years.

Contents

ACKNOWLEDGEMENTS

ACKNOWLEDGEMENTS USUALLY END with a warm and heartfelt expression of gratitude to the author's spouse for wise advice and unfailing support. I'd like to begin my acknowledgments by thanking my wife, Maria, who has lovingly carried the burden of our large family not only while I worked on this book, but also whenever I worked away in my "ivory tower." She provided sound advice when I was flailing and comfort when I was discouraged. Of course she provided unfailing love and warmth through it all.

Next I'd like to thank Bishop William Swing, a spiritual entrepreneur of the first order. He is the founder of the United Religions Initiative, the world's largest grassroots interfaith organization. Working with him over the last ten years has been a gift.

But this acknowledgement concerns my memoir. The bishop wrote a memoir and finished it while I was still shuffling papers for this one. He was helped in his efforts by a highly effective writing coach and editor. The bishop's writing coach, Sandra Gary, came on the scene when I was knee-deep in manuscripts that covered events throughout most of my life. Focusing the memoir on the formative period from 1938 to 1941, we developed the material over the next two years. Then she guided me through the publishing process. What you hold in your hand is very much a product of her professional skills.

Sally W. Smith lent her considerable editorial expertise to do an excellent job not only editing copy but also making suggestions for substantively reorganizing the material to produce a better flow of the narrative. I am grateful for that.

Barbara Geisler joined the editorial team as the graphic designer whose talents put the book in its final form.

I am deeply indebted to Sandra and grateful to her for introducing me to Sally and Barbara, whose talents greatly helped bring the work to a happy conclusion.

I am also indebted to many family members and friends. Some European cousins provided or confirmed family information. And some cousins there, family members here and friends had the opportunity to preview the first third of the book. Their support and suggestions were invaluable and I thank them for that.

FOREWORD

IN THE BACK OF THE TOP SHELF OF A HALL CLOSET, we found a black woven plastic bag. It was 1993. My mother had died, and my wife, my sister, Elizabeth, and I were cleaning out her apartment, the same apartment into which our family had moved in 1943.

The plastic bag contained a packet of letters in Mutti's native German. That did not surprise me. My mother was a prodigious letter writer, a common practice in the days before the Internet and easy transatlantic calls. My mother's parents and her extended family lived in Europe and she wrote them and a network of friends regularly. I put the black plastic bag aside for another day.

In the closet we also found a musty cardboard box containing a typed manuscript in English. A letter with the manuscript suggested it was written around 1951. That was also not surprising. When Elizabeth and I were in high school, my mother decided to complete her education and attended Hunter College. She was always a great storyteller, and in college began writing. She worked on a small magazine and wrote, under various names, a good deal of the text in the magazine. Eventually she wrote *Music for God: A Portrait of the Life of Anton Bruckner*, a biography of the Austrian composer, which was published in 1951 by Philosophical Library press. The manuscript we found was several inches thick, and I put that aside as well.

Ten years later, after I had retired, I decided to look at the letters again. I found that they all dated from 1938 and, although my German was limited, I sensed that they were more than just family news and gossip. With a German dictionary at hand, I started to work through them. It was daunting. I could understand much of the routine material and I could grasp the closing messages, sending hugs and kisses, often a thousand kisses. Eventually, I realized that professional translators could remove that burden and allow me to immerse myself in the story.

Another challenge arose. My father used a typewriter and his letters were usually dated. My mother's letters were hand-written and undated. I had the job of studying the context to put them in the proper sequence. It became a labor of love.

When I examined the contents of the bag more carefully, I saw that it also contained documents, most dating from 1938 and many dealing with my father. Once translated, the letters and documents together revealed a period fraught with tension and danger, as Hitler rose to power and my parents felt they must leave Austria. My father had made his way to Hungary, while my mother remained in Austria to try to obtain the necessary emigration permit. Both of them were addressing the even more difficult challenge of finding a place to emigrate to.

In addition, what slowly unfolded in the letters was the love my parents shared and how it supported them through terribly trying times. I learned how important they were to each other and how important my sister and I were to them as well. They made great personal sacrifices to keep all four of us together.

When I began, I had thought to tell my story as I remembered it. Slowly, the more interesting and emotionally resonant story was that of my parents. Fortunately, their letters and my mother's manuscript provided the material needed for this memoir.

Two questions arose as I was reflecting on the material. Why had my mother kept all that material for more than fifty years?

My wife's womanly answer is that the letters were love letters and they meant too much to my mother to just throw them away. A small voice says yes, that's a good response,but perhaps my mother kept them (and the documents) in the expectation that they would be found and then her children and grandchildren would know more details of the hazards they faced in 1938. I was 6 years old in 1938; Elizabeth was a year and a half younger. We knew the arc of the story, but my parents had spared us the grim details of their struggle. Nor had we ever discussed the urgent reason for their departure.

The second question is based on the fact that the letters were written in Europe in 1938 and were found in New York. Did my parents carry the letters with them all the time in their sojourn in Brazil and then to the United States? Elizabeth proposed an alternative, that perhaps the letters written in Europe stayed in Europe when my parents left and were retrieved on one of the several trips they made to visit family after the end of World War II. That makes a good deal of sense, the only oddity being that some of the letters in the black bag were actually written or received while my parents were in Brazil.

Working with the materials has been a bittersweet blessing. It has been a blessing to have come to know my parents as loving adults struggling with the grave challenges they faced. It was bittersweet that I had not known them as well while they were alive. I had seen them as good parents but missed the much deeper and more satisfying adult dimensions.

A well-known writing teacher, William Zinsser, entitled one of his books on writing memoirs *Inventing the Truth*. It's a catchy title since it appears self-contradictory. Yet I have to admit that there were gaps in the material or questions regarding the sequence of letters. You pause, reflect, and then, "invent the truth" that you believe occurred at that time. There were such occasions in this memoir.

Writing this memoir has been a gratifying exercise. I hope you enjoy it as well.

1

OUR WORLD CHANGES

The Man on the Balcony

We could see Hitler from the park where we played. He stood on a high balcony on Vienna's City Hall acknowledging the cheers of an enthusiastic crowd in the plaza below. It was March 15, 1938. I was 6 years old.

German troops had marched into Austria two days earlier, greeted by flag-waving crowds. The Anschluss — the combination of Austria and Germany into one country — had just been announced. Now hundreds cheered as Hitler looked down with a triumphant smile.

Those cheering saw him as a heroic figure who embodied their aspirations for respect and recognition, for pushing back against the German leaders who had cravenly (in Hitler's view) accepted an armistice to end the First World War and then were forced to accept the punitive peace of the Treaty of Versailles in 1920. That treaty had dismembered the Austro-Hungarian Empire, an empire that had ruled a large part of Europe for generations. The treaty had also put crushing reparation payments on the defeated nations.

Now Hitler had brought Germany and Austria together, something forbidden by the treaty. It was one more instance of Hitler's standing up to the allies who had imposed that burdensome treaty. It was also, in the eyes of those now looking at Hitler, another step in their return to the glories of the past. Many believed that the "Greater Germany" brought on by the Anschluss would restore their nation to its "rightful" place in the world.

Hitler had an eye for theater and it was no accident that he chose the ceremonial center of that earlier empire as the first place to greet the public in Vienna. From his vantage point, he looked across the broad Ringstrasse and saw, beyond our park, the stately Hapsburg palace, with its symmetrical lawns and gardens. It evoked the grandeur of the past. To Hitler's right and left, along the Ringstrasse with its handsome trees, stood grand government buildings and the mansions, indeed private palaces, of the wealthy.

The Austro-Hungarian Empire may have been destroyed and the grandeur of Vienna as the imperial capital may have dimmed, but still, the Ringstrasse and the Habsburg complex reminded the Viennese of what had been. Hitler's audience was not limited to the crowd of Viennese gazing up in admiration; Hitler had been greeted by large crowds as he made his triumphant way to Vienna, with German flags flying from most houses along the way. An air of euphoria gripped the country.

Eventually, the excitement of that day with its cheering crowds and waving flags dimmed as people returned to work and chores, and children returned to school. But the sense of optimism and patriotism brought on by the Anschluss and Hitler's appearance continued for many.

When we came to the park the next day, the older boys raised their right arms and shouted, "Heil Hitler." We youngsters returned the salute, yelling "Heil Hitler" to prove our commitment and pride. "Line up," the older boys commanded, standing side by side. We lined up behind them and then we all marched proudly around the park.

Back home, I cut a picture of Hitler out of a magazine, colored it with my crayons, and taped it to the window by my bed. I put a few trinkets in front of the picture, making a sort of altar. I looked forward to going to the park every day, as I always had, but now I wanted to march with the other boys and give salutes just like the soldiers. The German flags hanging from most buildings showed that many were caught up by the same spirit.

The Weisers in Vienna

Mutti, my mother, took my sister and me to the park almost every day. We walked hand in hand down to the corner, where the bustling avenue broadened into a wide boulevard that gave you a broad vista of the sky, the palace, and the park. We loved the Volksgarten (the People's Garden), with its pebbled walks, banks of roses and manicured lawns. A small replica of a Greek temple stood to one side. Benches allowed adults to sit and chat while we children ran around and had fun. The small temple was just the right size for us to chase around and play hide-and-seek. We used the steps in front for many games. Our mothers dressed us in "city" clothes, but we still managed to run and shout and laugh.

We lived only a few blocks from the park in a large, sunny apartment on the second floor. Papa, my father Arthur Geza Weiser, a doctor, had his office and examining room at home, adjacent to the formal living room, which doubled as a waiting room for patients. Papa was a urologist who headed the urology department at one of Vienna's major hospitals. He had a distinguished reputation and patients even came from other countries to consult with him. Papa was a man who respected others; he saw that others had value and acted accordingly; he was unfailingly polite and gentlemanly. Politeness usually attracts a comparable response and so Papa's life moved in an atmosphere of positive interactions. He made good friends and worked at keeping those friendships. His treatment of others

as beings of value also made him a good leader, because others appreciated the dignity he accorded them. An intelligent man, Papa
worked hard at his studies and his profession; he had twenty papers
published in peer-reviewed journals and steadily rose to positions
of higher responsibility. Papa was also disciplined, as we can see
from both his professional success and his life-long commitment
to playing a musical instrument, first the clarinet and later the flute,
at a high level of competence, with the daily practice that requires.
Papa enjoyed the satisfaction of challenging physical endeavors: He
rowed and had sculls in a shelter behind our country house, and he
was an avid hiker.

Mutti (Theresa, known as Resa) matched several of Papa's traits.
She was also a musician, in her case a pianist of public concert qual-
ity, which meant long hours of daily practice at the grand piano in
our living room. Playing at a high level brings its own reward, but it
has to be fueled by the effort of practice. A strong, healthy woman,
Mutti also enjoyed challenging physical activities and, like Papa,
enjoyed hiking. Like many women of her generation she had not
attended college, but on graduation from high school began helping
at her family's restaurant and pursuing her musical career.

I was known as Hansi, a nickname for Johann. My full name is
Johann Wolfgang Anton Maria Weiser. I was told that I had been
named after Johann Wolfgang von Goethe, the great German writer.
Anton was my maternal grandfather's name; many people, including men, were given the name Maria, the name of the Virgin Mary,
to honor her. At preschool and kindergarten in Vienna, I showed
early flashes of a strong intellect. Like Mutti, I had a vivid imagination. I tended to be a bit of an introvert, like my mother, who spent a
lot of time thinking to herself. Brown-haired and dark-eyed, I con-
trasted with the light blond hair and light green eyes of my sister
Lisl (short for Elizabeth), who was a year and a half younger than I
was. Beautiful and lively, Lisl was an uncomplicated child who en-

joyed life and all around her and saw everyone as a friend.

Lisl and I shared a bedroom that faced the street. We played in our room and in the large dining room next to it, which also served as a family room. That room had a large chandelier, well anchored in the ceiling, as I demonstrated once. The maid cleaning the chandelier went to answer the door and left the ladder unattended. When she came back, I was hanging on the chandelier. The dining room had two large windows facing Kirchengasse (Church Street), which took its name from the church at the end.

We had a live-in housekeeper to help with cooking, cleaning, and watching Lisl and me. Sometimes she invited Lisl and me into her small room next to the kitchen and played the zither for us, which we loved.

One of our regular walks was to the home of an older lady with whom Papa had boarded while he attended medical school. The lady had a bird in a cage. As a treat when we visited, she would put the birdcage on the windowsill, open its door, and allow the bird to fly outside to the park facing her apartment. To our delight, the bird always returned before we left.

Sundays brought the highlight of the week when we would go to my grandparents' house for lunch. My maternal grandparents, Anton and Theresa Metzger, were known to us as Opapa and Omama. They lived in an apartment over their restaurant, an establishment that had been in the Metzger family since 1826 and was, I believe, the oldest restaurant in Vienna. Its name, Zum Guten Hirten (At the Good Shepherd's), carries a religious connotation, not surprising since Austria was a Catholic country and religion permeated much of life. A large Catholic church stood across the busy street that ran by the restaurant, its original bright yellow softened by the years to a warm sunshine hue.

Omama and Opapa's bedroom had a kneeler for praying. I always assumed it was Omama's. But Opapa was a devout man. He

Opapa Anton Metzger in 1914.   *Omama Theresa Metzger in 1914.*

was my godfather, and on the occasion of my baptism gave a warm toast invoking heavenly blessings for me. He wrote it down and gave a copy to Mutti to pass on to me.

When Opapa saw us enter the restaurant, he would smile and come toward us. He was a short, bald man with a round, sunny face and a full mustache. He would give Mutti a kiss on the cheek, Lisl and me a warm smile and a small pat on the cheek; he would shake Papa's hand. "I'm so happy that you are here. I'll see you upstairs in a few minutes," he would say. Opapa's warm, friendly, nice way with people made him a good restaurant host. Mutti said that when she was a girl, she often turned to him when she needed special help or support. She said he was the first person she went to see to seek permission to marry Papa.

We would make our way into the middle of the restaurant, walking under low plaster ceilings and under stone arches that divided one section from another. Passing the large cash register with its many buttons and bulging front, we would climb up the narrow stone stairway that led from the restaurant to the apartment above. Through a large window we'd peer into the kitchen, seeing clouds of

Omama and Opapa Metzger's restaurant, Zum Guten Hirten,
around the turn of the twentieth century.

steam and women in white work tops and aprons working among large kettles. Sometimes we'd see Omama there. She supervised the kitchen, while Opapa handled the front and the guests.

Lisl and I had our own small table for lunch in the anteroom of the apartment, from which we could see into the dining room with its long table where the adults ate. We sat by a window and could look down on diners in the open-air patio sheltered in the wings of the building. Our traditional Sunday lunch was Wiener schnitzel and green peas, a Viennese specialty.

Next door to the restaurant, a lively open-air market hummed from dawn until mid-afternoon. Omama rose very early to go to the market for the freshest fish and vegetables. She was a woman who made up her mind quickly and ran the kitchen with a firm hand. I was told that when she married Opapa, she went to her mother-in-law and said, "Thank you. I will take over now." And she ran the kitchen from then on.

Mutti quoted Omama as often saying, "I know what I am doing and why." She was loving to us but generally no-nonsense. In the photograph opposite, to me the most noticeable aspect is her determined stride.

*Lisl and Hansi walking with Omama
on a street in Vienna in 1938.*

She recruited young women from the country to serve on staff. Their mothers were happy to send them because Omama watched the girls carefully. And when the girls left service to return home or to marry, Omama gave them a cookbook written in her own hand. She also gave one to Mutti when she married. Our family still treasures it.

My grandparents' home had a large empty room that my cousins and I used as a playroom. It was well maintained, and I assume it was used from time to time for private dinners for guests. Mutti told us that it had also been a playroom for her and her brothers and sisters. Sometimes when we played there, an older woman with beautiful white hair walked in slowly and watched us with a smile. Her name was Weibi. She had been the governess for Mutti and her siblings, and though they had long grown up and left, she still lived with my grandparents.

Omama and Opapa Metzger had a large family — four boys and three girls, plus an orphaned niece, Berta, that they raised as their own. Mutti was the sixth child, and second of the three daughters. I have little memory of most of my uncles and aunts, but I have learned a bit about them. Three of my uncles fought in both world wars. Uncle Toni (Anthony) was a spiritual person who never married. Josi (Joseph) was a healthy, strong character. The story is that during the Second World War, he was at the front. During a lull in the fighting he began to play his violin. A Russian sharpshooter shot toward the sound and badly injured him, but he survived. He married but never had any children. Alfons (Fonsus), the most energetic of the bunch, unfortunately did not survive the war. He was shot on the Russian front and is buried by a small orthodox church somewhere in Russia. He had three children: Alfons, a real estate developer known as the Trump of Austria when that was a compliment; Joseph, who was the sports editor and lead sports reporter for Vienna's largest newspaper; and Hedi, who owned and ran a *heurigen*, a neighborhood bistro, so called because it is allowed to sell its own new wine. She had a small vineyard outside Vienna. I know little about my uncle Fritz, but one of his two

Three of Theresa's brothers — Toni, Josi, and Fonsus Metzger —
during World War I.

sons is a highly successful organist who is choir director and organist at the Salzburg cathedral. He regularly gives concerts and is a professor at the Salzburg music academy (Mozarteum University Salzburg).

Aunt Gusti (Augusta) married an engineer and lived in Linz. She was somewhat sickly; a thin and drawn woman. She had three children, two boys and a girl. Her husband was strongly in favor of the union of Austria with Germany and probably belonged to the Austrian Nazi party. I met Berta when I visited in the 1980s. She was a warm and vibrant woman, but I have no recollection of her as a child. We were close to the family of my aunt Rieda (Maria). A woman who liked order and was strict but fair, she was the mother of Ernst and Hans Huber. Hans was almost exactly my age and we often played together; he was my closest friend.

Sometimes we visited Omama's mother, my great-grandmother, Mariana Nockeis Marcher. She was a very old lady who lived down a side street near my grandparents' restaurant. Her apartment was very quiet and we walked in carefully when visiting. Great-grandmother sat at the far end of the sitting room in a red velvet armchair with a white doily behind her head. She wore a dark dress of a heavy fabric that reached to the floor, and a lace cap on her head. We learned to walk respectfully up to her, say hello, and kiss her hand. One day, I was told she ate a good lunch, sat down in her armchair, fell asleep, and never woke up. It seemed a wonderful way to die.

The First Consequences of the Anschluss

T he visit of Adolf Hitler and the Anschluss marked the beginning of a process that would put increasing pressure on our familiar daily life. History unfolded around us and increasingly swept us up in its turmoil, month by month.

At first, life seemed to me unchanged. We continued to go to the park every day, and have Sunday lunch at Omama and Opapa's as often as before.

For other inhabitants of Vienna, things were very different. After the Anschluss, the Nazis began rounding up anyone who had opposed the union with Germany or who had a prominent role in civil society. They arrested newspaper editors, military officers and other civic leaders — anyone who might be a rallying point for opposition to the Nazis. Early in his political career, Hitler had loosed thugs on political opponents, but as the Nazis gathered more political power, they often imprisoned opponents. As historian Martin Gilbert wrote in *A History of the Twentieth Century, Volume Two: 1933-1951*, the Nazis "had a ruthless readiness to deploy police powers. They created an atmosphere of uncertainty and fear to silence any opposition."

On March 17, two days after we saw Hitler at City Hall, the Nazis purged the university, dismissing key professors. They were much rougher with other perceived opponents. Several members of the Gestapo, Hitler's secret police, took Franz Rothenberg, the board chairman of Austria's leading bank, for a car ride. They threw him out of the moving car, killing him, according to Giles MacDonogh, writing in *1938: Hitler's Gamble.*

The first train to the Dachau concentration camp left Vienna on March 31, less than a month after Hitler's appearance. That train contained 151 people, chosen because they held positions of power and authority in the Austrian state and were potential opponents of the Nazis. One witness cited in MacDonogh's book described a "work party" at Dachau about that time that included "two ambassadors, three ministers, a state secretary, a senior judge, a state prosecutor, the mayor of Vienna, a general, a colonel and three majors, two university professors, some senior police officers, two prominent Viennese lawyers, and a number of well-known journalists and authors."

Vienna's Jews had reason for grave concern as they saw the Nazis rounding up potential opponents. They could not help but be aware that the Nazis had been cultivating an increasingly virulent anti-Semitism in Germany. Vienna's Jews had a high profile and played a remarkably disproportionate role in Vienna's professional life: They were about 10 percent of the city's population, yet 85 percent of Vienna's lawyers were Jewish; so were 80 percent of the newspaper proprietors, and 75 percent of the bankers. Fifty percent of Vienna's doctors were Jewish.

As Hitler saw it, Germany's problems were due not only to the Treaty of Versailles but also, in his words as quoted by MacDonogh, to the "anti-national activities of Marxists and Jews." He denounced them as traitors and agents of the national collapse of 1918. In his view, the righting of Germany's wrongs demanded the renewal of Germany's culture by purifying its racial stock through cutting out "non-Aryan" elements. He had, as MacDonogh noted, "a personal and pathological hatred of the Jews whom he believed to threaten Germany's Aryan racial purity." His blunt solution, "The Jews must go."

In Germany, in 1935, Nazi anti-Semitism had been codified in the Nuremberg laws, designed to crush Jews economically. Jews could no longer own property, practice professions or employ others. Nor could they marry an Aryan. They were even forbidden from entering public parks. It was a devastating blow to people who had lived all their lives in Germany and whose ancestors had been there for generations. It was so unexpected that many German Jews could not bring themselves to believe it.

Many of Vienna's Jews worried whether the same fate might befall them.

On March 16, a black limousine pulled up to Nazi headquarters in Vienna. Two men stepped out. They would become infamous. One was Heinrich Himmler, head of the Gestapo; the other was Adolf Eichmann, a mid-level functionary, who would become the architect of the Holocaust. The two men were to take charge of handling Vienna's Jews. Eichmann was responsible for the legal emigration of Jews from Austria. His job was to implement Hitler's dictum that "the Jews must go" and to move Jews out of Austria as quickly as possible [MacDonogh].

Hermann Göring, the second most powerful man in Germany, complicated Eichmann's task. He qualified Hitler's directive that the Jews must go with the requirement, "But they will kindly leave behind their money, which they have only stolen" [MacDonogh].

The task of ensuring that Jews left all their assets behind, and of finding hidden assets, was assigned to Himmler and the Gestapo. They had a network of 800 spies for their work, and they were also significantly helped by the willingness of some Viennese to denounce others. MacDonogh says, "There was a mythical Viennese saint called 'Sancta Denunziata.' ... [It] was reckoned that a quarter of all investigations came from information provided by private persons."

Eichmann moved quickly to his task. Two days after he arrived, he participated in a raid on the offices of the Israeli Cultural Society (the IKG), an umbrella organization for over 100 social welfare groups operated by Jews in Vienna. The raid gathered lists of names of people active in the IKG, which became lists of people to be moved out. The IKG itself was dissolved.

Country Houses

————

Meanwhile, from my perspective as a 6-year-old, our family's life continued as usual. We had a weekend cottage in the country on the Danube River at Kuchelau, an hour's drive from Vienna. Every day that we were there, Mutti would take Lisl and me down the path to the river for a swim. The Danube had a strong current, but we swam behind a long stone breakwater that had been built parallel to the shore and provided calm water for swimming and rowing. Papa kept two rowing sculls in a shed behind the house.

Some swimmers did brave the current of the Danube. Mutti told me that my uncles and their friends would take a train upstream from Vienna, put on bathing suits, put their clothes in a waterproof floating bag, and float back down to town with the current. She also spoke happily of boating down the river with Papa on spring days when the trees on the riverbanks were in full bloom.

One day, Mutti, Lisl and I swam out from shore, and when we returned, Lisl discovered that the air had escaped from her waterwings. She felt a moment of terror, but it was swept away by the thrill of realizing she had been swimming on her own. Other swimmers had real problems. Once a man almost drowned and had to be hauled out of the water and given artificial respiration. Mutti tried to shield me from the sight, gently guiding me away, but I glimpsed an almost bluish cast to the man's body. It was an arresting sight.

On our way to the water, we walked by the house of a lady who had a wonderful butterfly collection that we were sometimes allowed to see. Several large glass cases contained beautiful specimens pinned in place. But what intrigued us about the lady was that Mutti said she had burned holes into her eyes by looking at the sun through binoculars. I was fascinated. I tried not to stare, but it was hard not to try to see the holes.

Most days in Kuchelau Mutti would give me a coin and send me to buy a cucumber from a farmer who had a small truck farm across the road. Thinly sliced cucumbers with a little vinegar, paprika and sugar were one of my favorite dishes. It was fun to go over to the farm and see the long straight lines of mounded earth as he prepared for planting, and the lines of vegetables that had sprouted and were growing. Strawberries grew in a patch behind the house, and we enjoyed looking for, and eating, the small berries hiding under the leaves.

Kuchelau holds many memories for me. It's where I learned to whistle, a big accomplishment that I raced upstairs to share with Papa because he had often coached me in how to whistle. I remember that one day gypsies camped with their caravans by a copse of trees not far from our house. I had heard that if gypsies saw you, they would capture you and take you away, but the fascination was powerful. I crawled carefully through some high grass until I could see the caravans clearly. My heart was pounding; I decided I was close enough. And I remember standing on the small balcony outside my parents' bedroom with Papa where we would marvel at the stars together. Papa enjoyed astronomy and had built himself a small telescope.

Every April of my life brought visits to Omama and Opapa's country house in Mühlberg, a short drive outside Vienna, not far from our place at Kuchelau. The old house was full of marvels, including a large closet we used for playing hide-and-seek. On sunny

*Omama and Opapa Metzger celebrating an anniversary
on the deck of their country house in Muhlberg.*

spring days, my grandparents would sit on the open deck, bundled up, playpens at their feet, enjoying the grandchildren around them. I always loved toddlers and playing with these little cousins.

And there were many cousins. Most of Omama and Opapa's children now had children of their own. My cousin Hans was also nicknamed Hansi, so I was Weiser Hansi and he was Huber Hansi. We played together whenever we could.

In Omama's back yard, a large tree had been pruned over the years so that its thick trunk was crowned by five or six well-spaced branches. They formed a natural tree house where Huber Hansi and I would spend hours. Omama had a shed in the backyard, where she kept a goat because she liked goat's milk. The property also had a long sloping meadow where we sledded and skied in the winter.

Our Family Feels the Pressure

As our pleasant life continued in April of 1938, the Nazis tightened their political grip by holding a plebiscite in Austria to approve the union with Germany. The vote was 99 percent in favor. There is evidence that negative votes were never counted. Still, there is little doubt that a majority of Austrians favored the Anschluss.

The same day of the plebiscite, April 10, the government adopted a new tax. Any person who wanted to emigrate from the country and who exceeded a defined level of wealth had to pay the new emigration tax of 25 percent before leaving [MacDonogh].

The search for assets stepped up. Jews, men or women, married to non-Jews now had to declare assets above a stated limit, whether held in Austria or abroad. The government also required a new permit for the transfer of a business from a Jew to a non-Jew.

In 1938, the Jewish Passover was celebrated from April 23 to April 26, with the 25th and 26th falling on the weekend. Jews who went to enjoy Vienna's large park, the Prater, were targeted for public humiliation. They were forced to spit in each other's faces. Some were forced to run around with their hands up and others were stripped and beaten, among them the 66-year-old chief rabbi. A Jewish general, while still wearing his Austrian army uniform, was made to wash the pavement [MacDonogh]. Similar hostile and aggressive incidents were being played out almost every day on the streets of the city. For instance, sometimes those being made to wash a sidewalk were given buckets containing water mixed with lye, so that their hands were badly burned. Street hooligans were having their day. As historian MacDonogh put it, "The populace relished the public shows of degradation; countless crooks from all walks of life, either wearing party uniforms or merely displaying improvised swastika armbands, applied threats and extortion on a grander scale."

The response to the violence could be tragic. According to historian Martin Gilbert in *A History of the Twentieth Century, Volume Two*, "On the night of March 19, sixty people killed themselves. In the weeks that followed that number rose to more than a hundred a day. ... Industrialists, professors, doctors, lawyers, civil servants, writers, journalists — people whose names were well-known and whose patriotism and liberal outlook was an integral part of interwar Austria — killed themselves rather than submit to incarceration and torture."

As Papa and Mutti saw the terrible repression of Vienna's Jews, they grew increasingly alarmed. They knew something about our family's background of which I had no inkling. Hints of that background arose as I grew older, but it took fifty years for me to confirm the truth. Papa's parents and grandparents were Jewish.

We were all Catholic as far as I could tell. Papa had been baptized a Catholic as a boy. The members of Mutti's large family were active and well-known Catholics. Lisl and I had been baptized Catholics and were being raised in that faith. Our family, including Papa, attended church and observed Catholic holidays. But even though both of Papa's parents had been baptized Catholic years earlier, Papa's Jewish origin posed a grave risk for him.

There was a significant difference between the views of the Catholic Church and those of the Nazis. The church accepted as Catholic anyone who confessed the faith and was baptized. It did not matter what religion he or she had belonged to before. The Nazis, on the other hand, were focused on "racial purity." If your grandparents had been Jewish, as far as the Nazis were concerned, you were Jewish, baptized or not [MacDonogh].

One evening in April, Papa told Mutti that he felt they would have to find a way to leave the country. He feared that his family's background would come to light and put us all in peril. Mutti had been hesitant to raise the issue; it was too painful to think about. She loved her extended family and enjoyed seeing her children playing with their cousins and seeing her mother and father watching it all with delight. And Papa had built a fine practice. He had an excellent reputation, a fine position and a promising future. I'm sure she cried as she agreed with Papa.

The next Sunday, Mutti's siblings met with her at Omama and Opapa's restaurant. The siblings felt that, while Papa might have to leave, Mutti should stay because she was Aryan and Catholic. "This whole thing will blow over in a matter of months. Arthur can come back when things have settled down and life has returned to normal," they would have said.

Odd as it may seem to us today, many people held the view that Nazism would not last long. In *Last Waltz in Vienna*, author Robert Clare writes about his Uncle Paul, a highly decorated veteran of the First World War who witnessed the parades in the streets supporting the Anschluss. "He just refused to believe that the world we lived in today and the one we had lived in yesterday were poles apart. He was still as convinced as he had been for the last five years that Hitler was a passing phenomenon."

Mutti's family meant well, but she found their proposal hard to accept. It did not look to her like the Nazis were going to be out of Austria any time soon. Papa knew that anti-Semitism had long been a central Nazi idea. He doubted they were going to drop it.

Papa had to leave.

It would be a painful wrench for Mutti to leave Vienna, the only home she had ever known. But most of all she wanted to be with Papa and to keep her family together. She recognized that he had to leave; she would go with him.

My parents began to focus on the overarching and crucial goal of finding a way out. The letters they sent and received document their efforts and lay bare the pressure they were under and the emotional toll exacted.

They began the process of applying for permits to emigrate, hoping to go to the United States, England or Canada.

Struggling to Leave Austria

Getting permits to leave Austria was one hurdle. A more difficult barrier was obtaining permission from another country to enter, especially to become permanent residents and live and work there.

Austrian Jews were finding it even harder to find safe havens abroad than German Jews, who had begun to emigrate from Germany starting in 1933; with that head start, they had filled the scarce openings available.

Author MacDonogh cites Wolfgang von Weisl, writing for a Jewish organization in Paris on May 16, as saying, "Practically every European country has hastened to close its doors to Jews from Austria." For example, the British had relaxed their immigration rules some years earlier, but in response to the Anschluss, had adopted new entry restrictions on May 21. They feared an influx of Central European Jews. "Once they were in, it would be very difficult to send them back," wrote von Weisl.

On May 20, the Nuremberg laws were adopted in Austria, to be given full effect on August 1. My parents continued their efforts to find a place to emigrate to. They talked to friends, hoping to obtain the names of people abroad who might help their entry into other countries. They also made a parallel effort to approach agencies in Vienna and abroad whose mission was to help people seeking to emigrate. Most of those agencies had a religious affiliation. In Vienna, my parents spoke regularly with the Society of Friends, the Quakers, who had an affiliate office in England.

The good standing of my mother's family with the Catholic hierarchy also led them to seek and obtain a letter of recommendation from the Archbishop of Vienna, Cardinal Theodor Innitzer. The cardinal's recommendation would eventually prove important.

The Nazis continued their repression of Vienna's Jews. At the beginning of June, Jews were banned from public parks and gardens in Vienna. On June 14, measures were introduced that would lead the way for compulsory transfer of all Jewish businesses to owners approved by the Nazis [MacDonogh].

At the end of June, my parents received a certificate of good conduct from the police authorities, the first step in the emigration process. Still required were Austrian tax clearances and other approvals.

On July 9, according to historian Giles MacDonogh, a Quaker woman in Vienna wrote to a friend in London, "The situation here has become infinitely more acute. ... Practically all Jews were dismissed from their employment on July 1, without notice and given no compensation. ... All Jews are being given notice to leave their houses if they are living in municipal blocks of flats, and also those living in the better districts of Vienna are shortly to be moved out." Jews had been cleared out of their villas in the plush Hietzing district and moved into *Judenhauser* (Jewish housing) in the Leopoldstadt. Their former homes were to be had for a pittance [MacDonogh].

From July 6 to July 14, U.S. President Franklin D. Roosevelt called a meeting of thirty-two nations at the French town of Evian to address the Jewish refugee problem. The invitation stated that "no country would be expected to receive a greater number of emigrants than is permitted by its existing legislation." The United States immigration legislation was described as "highly restrictive" [Gilbert].

The Spectator, a London paper, editorialized, "It is an outrage to the Christian conscience especially that the modern world with all its immense wealth and resources cannot get these exiles a home and food and drink and a secure status." A mainstream British Catholic newspaper wrote on July 14, "We cannot stand aside … and fail to respond to their cry for help." But no action was taken. A *Newsweek* correspondent reported from Evian, "Most governments represented acted promptly by slamming their doors against Jewish refugees" [Gilbert].

A German newspaper crowed, "Nobody wants them" [Gilbert].

By July 28, a third of Jewish property in Austria had been transferred to non-Jewish hands.

My father applied for admission to the medical school of the University of Edinburgh to qualify for practice in England. On July 18, 1938, the dean of the faculty of medicine at the university responded in a letter to my father, "I regret to state that it is not possible to admit you to this medical school for the purpose of obtaining a medical degree in this country. The number of applications which we have already received is greatly in excess of the number of places which we have available."

A friend wrote a letter introducing Papa to a Mr. Gerald Heller, a well-to-do rancher in western Canada. Mr. Heller generously accepted the challenge and jumped into action. He wrote a strong letter of support for Papa to the Canadian immigration authorities. On August 22, he received a reply from the Canadian commissioner of immigration, which he forwarded to Papa. The commissioner wrote, "Dr. Weiser has apparently very high qualifications, but I would point out that we are simply being inundated with requests for the admission to Canada of professional men from Continental Europe and to permit their entry would mean an extensive movement of Continental Europeans to this Dominion." The commissioner rejected the application.

In late July, a new and promising prospect appeared for my father from John Bruce, a satisfied and grateful patient, who was a senior officer at the Old East Africa Trading Company in London. Wanting to help, Bruce told Papa that his company had a branch in Kenya, where he believed European doctors were needed. The company's man in Kenya, Rudolf Loy, began the effort to bring my father there. Papa was willing to go. However, doctors who wanted to practice in Kenya, an English colony, had to pass a test administered in England.

Papa tried again to gain entry to England, this time with the prospect of moving to Kenya once the English requirements were met. In early August, he was advised by the registrar of the Royal College of Physicians in Edinburgh that his name had been placed on the waiting list for the "Triple Qualification Examinations." Since he was a graduate of "a recognized foreign University," he was not required to take the first examination. He was on the list to take the second examination. Unfortunately, the registrar noted, "there is no possibility of your being allowed to appear for examination before October 1940," more than two years away. The letter went on to specify that after passing the second examination, my father would be required to undertake twelve months' hospital practice at a recognized hospital in England. Then he would be allowed to take the third examination.

Papa would, I think, have happily done all that, but the issue was how to enter England and support his family during the extended period until the next examination. He wrote to a Mrs. Derenburg of the German Jewish Aid Committee in London asking for their help, pointing out that he was now on the waiting list for a test to be administered twenty-six months later. He wrote, "I need hospitality for this period. ... My wife and my two children can remain here [Vienna] for the intervening time, as the family of my wife will help them." He added, "Directly after my qualification, I shall leave England for Nairobi, Kenya Colony where Mr. R. Loy, Managing Director of the Kilimbini Coffee Curing Company, Mombasa will give me aid for settling there."

The Nazis continued to tighten their grip on Austrian Jews. On August 8, a decree was issued prohibiting Jews from practicing medicine. More than half of Austria's doctors were Jewish [MacDonogh]. The decree would also have a profound effect on my father if the authorities were to learn of his family background. The next day, August 9, Jews were required to leave apartments owned by non-Jews. The streets were quickly clogged with moving vans [MacDonogh]. On August 17, the Nazi party forced Jews to adopt the middle name of Israel, for men, and Sarah, for women. Jews were no longer allowed to use Gentile names [MacDonogh].

On August 20, the remaining organizations in Vienna dealing with Jewish matters were consolidated into the Central Office for Jewish Emigration, housed in the former Rothschild palace on the Prinz-Eugen-Strasse. Its aim was to expedite emigration [MacDonogh]. Mutti would become very familiar with the palace on Prinz-Eugen-Strasse.

In mid-August, the British press reported that 30,000 Jews had received permission to leave Austria but had no visas to enter another country. Those 30,000 Jews had worked their way through a daunting bureaucratic maze to obtain that permission to leave [MacDonogh].

Papa Is Declared a Jew

Mutti and Papa thought they had been working to leave Austria as members of the general public, not as members of a harassed and persecuted group.

That was about to change.

A small piece of local mail arrived at our apartment. It was a postcard, dated August 16, 1938, from the Registry of the Jewish Cultural Community in Vienna. It read, "It has been confirmed, based on information received, that Dr. Arthur Weiser, born on March 19, 1896 in Budapest, Hungary, is a full Jew."

What "information" had been "received" and from whom, we never knew. A sad suspicion hung in the air that it had been a member of the extended family. It did not matter. The card spoke for itself, its authority authenticated by a formal seal of the Nazi government.

The card was small but its implications were huge, profound and devastating. The Nuremberg laws and other anti-Semitic governmental actions now applied fully to my father. It did not take long for our family to feel the impact. Years later, Mutti told me that people would write "Jewish establishment" next to the front door of the building, because my father's office was there. She would wash it off the next morning only to find it written again overnight.

For me, the first effect was that Mutti took down the picture of Hitler that I had taped on my window. She told me that a neighbor

This is the document stating that Arthur Weiser was a "full Jew."

had objected to it. I thought perhaps it was because I had colored it with crayons. I cut out another picture of Hitler from the newspaper, left it uncolored, and put it up again. My mother quickly removed it and said, "Do you want us to go to jail?" I did not understand that. People went to jail because they did something wrong and I wondered why putting up a picture of Hitler would be wrong.

Then I had a real blow. We went to the park as usual. Two of my good friends were playing there. I ran up to them but they turned their backs on me and walked away. Sometimes they'd look like they wanted to play but then they'd glance at their mothers and stop. They were like brothers to me and now they were ignoring me, shunning me. I was confused and hurt.

Even at Omama and Opapa's apartment, something wasn't quite right. When other cousins were there and we'd head into the large playroom, they'd look at their mothers as though they needed permission to play with me. Happily they always came to play, but I did hear one of my aunts say, "It's okay in the house; you just can't do it outside."

Papa's new legal status gave great urgency to my parents' letter-writing campaign and to finding a way out.

Papa Leaves

Less than a month after the fateful postcard arrived at our apartment, three of Papa's friends, also doctors, were arrested and taken away. He realized he had no time to lose.

Late in the afternoon of September 13, Papa put on a light overcoat and his homburg and went to the train station, carrying a small overnight bag. At the station, he bought a round-trip ticket to Budapest and then at the newspaper kiosk purchased a newspaper and a magazine. When the train to Budapest was announced, he quietly boarded the train.

In the past, this had meant a few hours of pleasant travel to Hungary. This time there was high risk and great tension. A cartoon in one of the pro-Nazi newspapers illustrated the concern. It showed a Jew being grabbed by a giant's hand at the frontier; its message: Jews could leave, but only with the document proving they had left their assets behind [MacDonogh].

Papa was traveling with his Austrian passport, which had not yet been stamped to identify him as a Jew. He had neither clearance to emigrate from Austria nor permission to live in Hungary. If questioned, he would have to lie convincingly.

He spent the next few hours trying to focus on the newspaper and the magazine he had bought, particularly whenever someone in uniform passed by his compartment. Then the two border guards, one German, the other Hungarian, entered the compartment. Fortunately, the Hungarian border guard came first to Papa. Papa gave him a big smile and spoke up in Hungarian, explaining that he was going to visit his mother. The guard accepted his story, reminded him that his visit could not exceed ten days, and stamped his passport.

The German border guard turned to Papa, who had relaxed a bit now that he had the first stamp in his passport. Papa had put his return ticket to Vienna in the passport. As he handed the passport to the guard, he took the return ticket out, in a deliberate way, to be sure that the guard saw it. The guard took Papa's passport and flipped through the pages. The pages showed several stamps of entries into Hungary and reentries to Austria, supporting the story of a visit. The German guard stamped Papa's passport. Danger averted.

Papa stayed on high alert for the rest of the trip. No other guards appeared, and he was grateful when the train pulled into the Budapest station. As soon as he stepped off the train, he wrote Mutti a postcard. "I am safely in Budapest. The border guards only did a light check, but I am exhausted." He added, "Continue to be as brave as you have been and keep reminding yourself that we still have a beautiful life ahead of us." That postcard was the beginning of the precious correspondence between my parents that my mother preserved.

Papa stayed that night at a small hotel near the train station. The next morning he boarded a local train for the short trip to the village of Máriabesnyő where his mother's small summer resort was located. Grandma Paula and Grandpa Koloman Weiser lived in an apartment in central Budapest. They bought a grand house as a country place in Máriabesnyő. I surmise that after Koloman died in 1924, Paula moved to the house full time and began to operate it as a resort for Budapest city dwellers. I knew it only as a resort. The government confiscated the property during the war. When I

Portrait of Grandpa Koloman Weiser   Portrait of Grandma Paula Holzmann
painted circa 1920.   Weiser painted circa 1920.

visited in the 1980s, the government had turned it over to gypsies, and in a sea of well-kept cottages, it was a slum. On the other hand, the house next door, which was a "twin," was preserved in its original condition and often used as a setting for movies, featuring its substantial size and large front veranda.

The train rolled slowly out of the cavernous Budapest station, picked up speed as it headed to the outskirts of the city, and finally reached full throttle as it broke out into open country. I imagine Papa looking out the window at the fields and cottages rushing by and thinking to himself, "How many times have I taken this ride to Máriabesnyő?" Happy trips as a youth; a trip in young manhood returning from the war with high hopes quickly to be dashed; and now, with enormous uncertainty about the future. He was not surprised that the Nazis had imposed the Nuremberg laws in Austria and were hounding the Jews. But it had brought so much more upheaval for him and his family than he could ever have imagined. And he still did not know how it would end.

He surely felt a sense of relief now that he was in Hungary where he had family and friends and where he was beyond the reach of the Nazis. Still, it was ironic. Fleeing to Hungary, he was reversing a trip he had made twenty years earlier.

A postcard featuring Grandma Paula's resort in Máriabesnyő.

Papa's Early Life

During the Great War (what we now call World War I) Papa had served almost three years as a lieutenant in the Austro-Hungarian Army on the Russian front. He had left as a boy of 19 and returned as a bone-tired 22-year-old, mature beyond his years. The fighting had been brutal and his job dangerous. He had spotted for the artillery, which meant he often had to crawl into no-man's-land between the front lines to guide artillery fire onto targets. He had been decorated three times for bravery.

The fighting on the Russian front had been fierce, but unexpectedly ground to a halt in the spring of 1918, as a result of the 1917 communist revolution in Russia. Lenin signed a peace treaty with Germany in order to concentrate on consolidating his power. Generals still loyal to the czar who were fighting on the Hungarian front moved their troops toward Moscow, bringing an end to the fighting on the front.

Papa made his way home. Sadly, his long and dedicated war service and the medals that recognized his heroism made little difference to the locals when he returned. Instead of being hailed as a war hero, he and others who had fought on the Russian front were now the targets of abuse. Communist revolutionaries had seized power in Hungary, just as Lenin and his cohorts had seized power in Russia. The new communist government saw the Russian people as allies; they were happy that the autocratic czar had been over-

Papa in the uniform of the Austro-Hungarian army during World War I.

thrown. Papa, it turned out, had not merely fought for a government that had been overthrown and for what turned out to be a losing cause. He had also fought the very Russians who were now seen by the new government as allies in the great workers' international revolution. Mutti told Lisl and me that on his return home, Papa was spat on by some of the new converts.

But the problems in Hungary were just beginning. The victorious Allies decided to dismember the losing Austro-Hungarian Empire and to allocate pieces of it to other countries. One large piece with Hungarian-speaking populations was included in the new nation of Czechoslovakia; another went to Romania.

The new communist government in Hungary was not prepared to accept dismemberment. It moved to reclaim the territories allocated to Czechoslovakia and successfully occupied Hungarian-speaking territories there. But when it went after Hungarian-speaking territories awarded to Romania, it ran into a buzz saw. The Romanians responded fiercely, fought their way into Budapest and, as victors, demanded huge reparations for their troubles. The communist government in Hungary collapsed.

A right-wing government came to power and unleashed the "White Terror." They sought out remnants of the communist government, people who had themselves been guilty of atrocities described as the "Red Terror." Among those remnants were Jews, since many had occupied senior positions in the communist government. It was a time of savage internal strife.

Hungary was Papa's home; it was where he had been born and had grown up in gentler times. His father Koloman was a banker who cultivated many acquaintances in the artistic community of Budapest. When a sculptor friend received a commission in the early 1900s to create a large monument to honor the Hungarian patriot and poet Mihály Vörösmarty, he requested that Papa sit as one of the models for this work. The multi-figure monument stands today as the centerpiece of Vörösmarty Square in Budapest, complete with Papa's likeness.

But that boyhood was far behind him in 1918, when strife-torn Hungary no longer seemed to offer any promise for a young man from a Jewish family, even though he had been baptized a Catholic

Papa modeling for a sculptor friend of the family.

Papa, his father Koloman, mother Paula, and sister
Elizabeth Weiser in Budapest in 1912.

as a boy. So Papa decided to look for better prospects in Vienna. Entering the University of Vienna's medical school in his new city, he began a new life.

Vienna in 1918 was still a grand city. It had been the seat of the Habsburg Empire, with Franz Josef reigning as emperor for sixty-eight years, from 1848 to 1916. During his reign, Vienna had been the cultural capital of German-speaking Europe. It boasted a long musical tradition and a heady intellectual climate, and as the long-time seat of empire, it still bore vestiges of the color and opulence of a large court. Franz Josef's death in 1916 marked the symbolic end of the empire.

The armistice in 1918 and the peace treaty following World

War I marked the political end of that grand, imperial world. After the peace treaty, Austria became a small remnant of the Habsburg Empire, with a quarter of its earlier population. Vienna must have worn a melancholy air.

Papa plunged into his studies, graduating from medical school in 1921. He did postgraduate work in surgery and trained for five years at the Surgical University Clinic under the tutelage of the distinguished Professor Hochnegg. Papa's father died of prostate cancer in 1924 and perhaps that was what made him decide in 1926 to specialize in urology. He was appointed first assistant to a doctor Papa described to us as the "world-famous urologist" Professor Victor Blum at the Sophie Hospital in Vienna. Papa also gave regular lectures and classes in English to members of the American Medical Association in Vienna. (Both of my parents spoke several languages. In addition to his native Hungarian, Papa spoke German from childhood; it was the language of government — Hungary was part of the Austro-Hungarian Empire — and a common second language for educated people. He learned English in school.)

Papa enjoyed medical research and within a few years after graduating from medical school, he began writing papers that were published in peer-reviewed professional journals. The early ones dealt with surgical topics, but after 1926, the topic was urology. In all, there were over twenty papers spanning a twelve-year period. In 1938, as he was seeking a position abroad, he wrote, "Without immodesty I can tell you that I am an experienced urologist, and as a result of my twenty scientific publications, have achieved a noteworthy reputation." Starting in 1933, Papa also acted as the consulting urologist for the Medical University Clinic of a Doctor Jagic. Papa worked with Professor Blum for ten years. In 1936 he was appointed head of the urology department at the Hospital of the Divine Savior in Vienna.

He was also able to enjoy a lively private life. My father was an accomplished amateur musician, excelling at both the piano and the clarinet. Later he took up the flute. A friend and fellow Hungarian, Willy Rózsavölgyi, played the violin and often joined him for musical duets on their free evenings. My father also met an attractive young woman who was an accomplished pianist and had given numerous public concerts. In time, she would become my mother.

Arthur and Resa

A s children we heard the story of how our parents met at a public swimming pool. They both enjoyed going there and discovered friends in common. One day, as they were sitting near each other, the young man who had brought my mother to the pool turned to her and said, "I'm sorry to say that I will not be able to bring you swimming in the future. I have accepted a job abroad and will be leaving soon." My father was within earshot and, not one to miss an opportunity, said to my mother, "If you permit, I can bring you next week." And so their romance began. Many years later, my father would describe his wife as "a beautiful animal" to my wife Maria.

We also heard that on one of my parents' early dates, my father arrived to pick up my mother and right away someone put a bucket in his hand, asking him to join a bucket brigade, to help put out a fire at my grandparents' restaurant.

My parents were both athletic and enjoyed walking. They hiked regularly in the Vienna Woods and, on their honeymoon, trekked through the Dolomite Alps, those magnificent, steep crags that feature rolling alpine meadows and challenging mountain trails. My father was also a dedicated sculler and sculled on the arm of the Danube near our summer cottage.

Eventually the time came when my father asked my mother to marry him. A worrier, she sat on a couch late into the evening, weighing the pros and cons. Her parents found her asleep on the couch in the morning.

She accepted my father's proposal and told her parents. Omama knew Arthur, but very little about his family. A cautious woman, she sent one of her sons to Hungary to do a background check. She told him, "If there are any red flags, call right away." So Mutti and the family waited. Three days later, the phone rang. Mutti's heart fell. Phone calls were rare in those days, and this call must be from her brother. Based on the instructions, it could not be good news.

Omama answered. It was, in fact, her brother. He said, "The news is very good. Arthur's family is well known and highly regarded. Everyone I spoke with had a good opinion of them. I called because I didn't want to make Resa wait until I got back."

The next step was for Omama, Opapa and Mutti to travel to Hungary to meet Papa's widowed mother. They had several hours on the train together and Omama used the time to tell Mutti that she was worried about the possible marriage. "Marriage has a lot of challenges and it's important that the girl and boy come from similar backgrounds," she said. The fact that the family was Hungarian concerned her. "I have nothing against Hungarians, but they have different customs, different foods, and a language that few people outside their country can speak. They are different. Why take on all those problems?" Then Omama came to the argument that had been brewing there quietly all the time: Arthur's family was Jewish. "We have always been a Catholic family and our religion is very important in our lives," she likely said. "One really should not marry outside one's religion. In those rare cases when people do it, all sorts of problems come up with children and the in-laws. You really should reconsider."

Mutti, near tears, could only say, "I really love Arthur and I know he loves me." Opapa had been silent. Now he smiled and put his arm around his daughter. He kissed her on the forehead and said, "Look how happy Arthur makes her." No more was said.

At Máriabesnyő, they made their way to the house of Grandma Paula. They could see a handsome woman with a silk scarf around her neck, standing on the open porch, smiling warmly. She threw open her arms. Omama could not resist the invitation; the two women embraced. My mother smiled. It was going to be all right. It became even better as the two women walked together to the kitchen, from which came the aromas of good cooking. Soon they were comparing cooking methods and recipes.

Mutti and Papa at their wedding in Vienna in 1930.

Papa in Hungary, Mutti in Vienna

Now, eight years later, Papa was coming back home to Máriabesnyő. In my imagination it was like this: He walked the short distance to his mother's place. He opened the gate and headed up the sandy lane between the lawns, around the circle of fall flowers, and up to the house. It had a welcoming air, with a broad veranda across the front and comfortable wicker chairs beckoning one to sit and relax. A cluster of small cottages for guests stood near the house. From the veranda Papa turned and looked below toward the village of Máriabesnyő nestled into the fold of the valley, and to the green hills beyond. It was a warm, lazy day and he wrote Mutti, "The September weather is gloriously beautiful."

Papa would have made his way toward voices in the kitchen and shared a long embrace with his mother. He would have given the cook a hug. Neni had been with the family since he had been a boy.

Once settled in his room, he wrote a letter to Mutti. He thought of Mutti and the burdens she was carrying. He was proud of her and admired her spirit in fighting through the bureaucracy. It reinforced his happiness in their marriage. He wrote Mutti, "In the meantime I will get a residence permit for six weeks, but it will get extended a couple more times. Maybe the Wagners [contacts in the United States] will be ready by then and we won't have to stay here for too long."

While Papa was gearing up in Hungary, Mutti was moving between two different worlds in Vienna — a world of people continuing their normal lives, and a world of people caught in a closing vise and desperate to escape.

Many Viennese sat at sidewalk cafés enjoying their afternoon coffee and watching shoppers scurrying by on busy avenues. Omama and Opapa's restaurant business was bustling and they were busy tending to it. Mutti's brothers and sisters were involved in their own lives. German soldiers patrolled the street and swastika flags flew, but most Viennese, like Mutti's family and friends, continued their everyday routines.

However, Mutti herself was deeply worried. Papa had avoided the immediate risk of internment. But his stay in Hungary could be only for a very limited time. Where and how would they find another country to take them in? And what did Mutti have to do to get the emigration visa? In addition, she faced the mundane but time-consuming tasks of closing the apartment, storing or selling furniture, and shipping out key pieces of Papa's medical equipment.

Mutti and Papa exchanged a continuing flow of messages of love and support as they struggled for answers. The letters provided the help and comfort they each needed from the other and reminded them of their love and their partnership in working to overcome the frightening prospects before them. As Papa wrote, "Thank you for your daily letters. The whole day is different when there is something from you in the morning mail." And Mutti wrote back, "Thank you for your letter today. It made my day."

Realizing how important his letters were to her, he wrote, "I am upset by the fact that you have not received any messages from me for two days. I have written you every day, though only a postcard on Saturday from Budapest. Regular mail leaves here in Máriabesnyő only once a day and I take the letters personally to the train ... so that nothing gets lost in the post office."

Mutti moved forward with determination to face the hurdles presented by the local bureaucracy. The Nazis wanted to get Jews out of Austria but bureaucrats were bureaucrats, punctilious and inclined to make any process onerous. All Mutti could do was to keep pushing ahead despite repeated rebuffs and setbacks. She had plenty of company. She wrote, "At the travel agency, I saw so many people who can't leave, simply because they can't retrieve a clearance that had already been processed by the tax authorities."

And the hurdles were daunting. As Giles MacDonogh described in his history, *1938: Hitler's Gamble*, "The process was Ulyssean. The first paper required was the *Steuerunbedenklichkeits-bescheinigung*, a certificate proving that all taxes had been paid. The process for obtaining it was as long and clumsy as the word itself. It involved visits to and payments to ... the directorate of the applicant's district [to obtain] a certificate of domicile ... next was ... the District Commissioner's department in the town hall; this was followed by the ... central tax office; and the tax office of the district where the applicant lived. If the forms had been filled in properly and the right sums paid, the applicant received his *Steuerunbeden-klichkeitsbescheinigung*, and could proceed to stage two."

MacDonogh continues:

> Stage two consisted of a visit to the *Devisen-stelle* where the Jews' assets were released and the department granted certificates of good conduct. The long queues outside both offices provided a means of making a little money for both the Nazis and unscrupulous Jews. ... Nazis with swastika armbands took 100-Reichmark bribes to issue numbered passes. ... Those waiting in the queues were sitting ducks: they could be picked out and sent off to clean up a barracks by SA-men [storm

troopers] or Hitler Youth boys. When they reached the top of the queue they were told the form was incorrectly filled in, and that they had to do it all again.

Stage three was the passport itself from the emigration office. You first went to the police station in your district ... to answer questions about the nature of the passport. ... Then the applicant went off to the emigration office in the Herrengasse, then to the passport office in the Wehrgasse, where the appropriate visas had to be obtained. ... The passport office in the Fifth District was one of the most feared stations of abuse and humiliation. ... On average, people waited for a day and a half before receiving their papers.

Fortunately, Mutti's experience at the passport office was better. "It took from 6:30 A.M. until 2:15 P.M.," she wrote, describing her wait at the passport office. "But the day after tomorrow I will receive my passport and the children will receive their 'mischling' ['mixed blood'] passports and they will be able to travel everywhere and return."

On the way home from the passport office she met the sister of a friend. "The sister lives with her cousin now," my mother wrote, "since her apartment has been confiscated." She ended her letter, "Farewell, my little bear. I am so happy that you miss me and I will come as soon as I can."

Back in Hungary, Papa was at work finding a way out and reported on September 16, "I received a promise that I will be able to stay for three months." If the promise were fulfilled, it would allow him to stay until late December. That seemed like more than enough time to figure a way out.

The next day, he visited his uncle Stefan, his father's brother. Stefan was a professor of chemistry at the University of Budapest, a senior adviser to the Ministry of Commerce and the author of a scholarly book on animal husbandry. Full of hope, Papa went to speak with Uncle Stefan to learn about his good friend's son-in-law, who was said to be an American diplomat who could provide invaluable help in dealing with the American immigration quota system. Sadly, it turned out that the man was in fact an employee of a shipping company and not in a position to offer any real help. It was just a false lead.

Papa wrote Mutti about the dead end. He also mentioned that he had visited the Chinese consulate in Budapest and learned that Shanghai was not accepting European physicians. On a happier note, he told Mutti that he had received a very nice note from Mrs. Bruce, the wife of John Bruce, the grateful patient, in England. Mrs. Bruce invited the whole family to stay with them and said she hoped that we would all be able to come to England. He ended his letter, "Please write soon to your always-thinking-of-you, somewhat-grumpy and many-time-hugging you Arthur."

The following week, on September 24, he wrote, "Since the British Prime Minister flew in to visit Hitler today, one can hopefully assume that everything will still work out okay." Certainly, British Prime Minister Neville Chamberlain thought so. When he returned home, he waved a copy of the agreement he had reached with Hitler and spoke of "peace in our time." Today, he is often vilified for his misjudgment and appeasement of Hitler. But Papa and many others at the time hoped, along with Chamberlain, that "everything will still work out okay."

One effort, one of several in the United States, foundered in late September. Papa received a letter dated September 13 from Dr. Ralph Walters, a senior doctor at Wisconsin General Hospital. Dr. Walters wrote that he had received Papa's letter, which he had reviewed with the chief of surgery at the hospital. He quoted that doctor's reaction, "What a tragedy. There have been at least twenty similar requests in the past months. There is nothing I can do." Walters included a clipping from a local paper stating that the clerk of the federal court there reported that applications were flooding in from local citizens seeking to bring in relatives and friends from Austria.

A potentially more hopeful possibility was Mrs. Rudolf Wagner, a relative of a friend, to whom he had referred in an earlier letter. She told Papa in a handwritten note, dated September 16, "There are many, many cases, hundreds of them, like yours, which all want help. So if you can be patient and wait, I am sure things will be all right. In the meantime I am doing all I can for you, and when people ask who I am to you, I answer that you are my niece's husband. So that you know now."

Mrs. Wagner told Papa to contact Miss Maud Rieff, who held a "very high position" with the company for which Mrs. Wagner's husband worked. Papa did, and Miss Rieff used her connections to obtain a letter of introduction from the office of Senator John Milton (a Democrat of New Jersey serving in 1938) to Garret G. Ackerson, Jr., the third secretary in the American Consulate in Budapest. Miss Rieff sent a copy of Senator Milton's letter to Papa.

Papa responded gratefully, reviewed his credentials for Miss Rieff and described the specific challenge he faced: Papa was Hungarian for U.S. immigration purposes and the U.S. immigration quota for Hungarians was filled for the foreseeable future. Hence he could not get a visa through the usual route of obtaining an affidavit of support. Rather, the only possibility seemed to be a specific offer of a job with a hospital or a medical school. No further correspondence from Mrs. Wagner or Miss Rieff appears in the collection of family letters, but a letter from the Committee for Catholic Refugees from Germany seems to follow up. It appears that Miss

Rieff reached out to them as a possible intermediary to find employment for my father.

Meanwhile, Papa had begun working in the medical office of a friend. He wrote Mutti, "The office is running well. I saw seven patients today, including three new ones."

Lisl and I Go to Hungary

About a month after Papa went to Hungary, Mutti decided to send us to Papa. She asked her sister-in-law, Tante Mitzi (Aunt Mitzi), wife of her brother Alfons, to take us. Lisl and I saw the trip as a fun visit to Grandma Paula. Mutti and Papa thought it would take only a few weeks to make arrangements for emigration and that Mutti could manage more easily without having to take care of us as well. Perhaps she also wanted to spare us the pain of being shunned in the park.

I always enjoyed train rides. I loved looking out the window at the passing fields, at the houses that backed up to the tracks with their neat little gardens at the back, at the animals in the fields. It was colorful and ever-changing.

We arrived in the cavernous Budapest station, enclosed at the top and open at the far end where the trains came and went. Steam from the locomotives floated in the air. Papa was there to meet us with open arms, "Hello, you little rascals. Give me a big kiss," he effused. He gave us both a long hug. Then he turned to Tante Mitzi, gave her a small kiss on each cheek, and thanked her.

Mitzi said, "I was happy to have time with the children. I'm not sure when I'll see them again." She leaned down to Lisl and me and gave us both a kiss and a good hug. We waved good-bye as Papa took us to our next train.

The train station in Máriabesnyő was an open platform on a

rise above the small village. From the platform we could look down at the houses and shops clustered together around a small church. We walked with some excitement and anticipation to Grandma Paula's resort. Grandma was waiting for us, and hugged and kissed us. She was more delicate in appearance than Omama, a little slimmer and with fine features. She ran a restaurant as part of the resort but it was smaller than Omama and Opapa's.

The next morning Papa said to me, "I've talked to the schoolteacher here and she says that you are old enough to attend. She is looking forward to meeting you. Why don't we walk down?" I did not speak Hungarian, but nobody seemed to think that was a problem, so I guessed I'd make my way.

Papa and I headed to school and Lisl came along, even though she was still too young to go to the first grade. We followed the lane toward the train station and then turned down a short lane that led to a pedestrian tunnel under the train tracks. I was glad Papa was with me. Even though I could see the opening at the other end, it seemed somehow spooky. We stepped out from the underpass into the sunlight. Open meadows rolled out on either side and before us lay the small village with its church, which attracted pilgrims from around Hungary. In the village, a short uphill climb from the house, we walked by a butcher shop. Suckling pigs hung from hooks in the shop window. I had not seen that before, and every day that I walked by, I looked up to see them.

The school building was a small structure where multiple classes shared only three classrooms. The teacher must have known Papa for a long time because they had a friendly conversation — in Hungarian of course. I was paying a lot of attention, trying to decipher what they were saying. Like many Hungarians, the teacher also spoke some German, and that helped me. And of course arithmetic worked the same in Hungarian as in German. So I began school in Hungary as Janos, the Hungarian version of Johann.

More Emigration Efforts

A friend of Papa's, whom he called "Director Hadjer," recommended that Papa reclaim his Hungarian citizenship, and offered to help. He and his wife invited Papa to lunch. He wrote, "It was so strange that I, as a poor immigrant, had a wonderful lunch at a luxury hotel." Being a citizen would remove the very real constraint on his permitted time in Hungary. Papa also thought that being a Hungarian citizen might perhaps improve his chances of meeting the immigration quota in the United States. Still, potential complications existed.

He wrote to Mutti, "Maybe you could ask the man at the British Consulate how I should best proceed about ... my new citizenship. That would be [good] to know since I don't want to offend them. Otherwise, I would never get an affidavit." But a problem could arise since current rescue efforts by organizations and governments were keyed to Austrian and German Jews. If he became a Hungarian, he might fall outside the scope of those efforts. Still, he thought it worth a try.

He also wrote to Mutti, "I will probably heed the advice from Fonsus [Mutti's brother Alfons] and not plan to live here indefinitely after the citizenship change. But first we have to put up with the next few weeks. We don't have much choice but to write letters and keep hoping."

The citizenship effort failed. He expressed his disappointment to a friend, writing, "After five weeks of multiple visits to government offices and some financial sacrifice for fees and expenses, the whole citizenship effort failed, and at the end of October, they even wanted to withdraw my residence permit. It was only thanks to a personal contact that I was able to reach Minister Frater, and then the agency renewed my residence permit until December 1." Later, just as the permit was expiring, it was extended to December 12.

As Papa met with friends and acquaintances, he wrote to Mutti, "the big question everyone is asking is if there will be war or peace." Hitler continued to expound Germany's "duty" to rescue the German-speaking population in the Sudetenland, now part of Czechoslovakia. There were concerns that if Hitler moved into the Sudetenland as he had moved into Austria, the Allies, invoking the Treaty of Versailles, might this time rise to the defense of Czechoslovakia and trigger a war. Czechoslovakia abutted Hungary; it was right next door. People were nervous.

Papa wrote about the effect the developments had on people in Hungary, "There is quite a bit of excitement noticeable today. There are constant calls from people in Budapest who want to come out to the country. Everybody has a different story and everyone seems irrational. I feel quite discouraged today because of the general fears about war. Let's hope this issue somehow resolves itself."

About the same time, Mutti had received a letter from England, which she sent to Papa. The letter was from a Ruth Mellanby, a friend of a friend and a concerned citizen who worked on our behalf with the German Jewish Aid Committee in London. She had learned of my parents' desire to come to England, "prior to going to the Colonies," as she put it. Mrs. Mellanby wrote that she was aware of the difficulty in getting entry permits but had a suggestion. She knew a Mr. Diblon who was a fellow of the Royal Horticultural Society and affiliated with the Botanical Gardens of Battle, Sussex. In order to help refugees in England, he employed them in a program of intensive vegetable growing. Mrs. Mellanby wrote, "He has room for another married couple and could take you in until you find that which you wish to do." She suggested that my parents send him their qualifications so he could apply for the necessary permits.

Papa was troubled. He responded to Mutti, "The Gardening School idea seems quite unusual. I am going to write to the lady that we are not going to take advantage of the opportunity; we might run into the problem that the [British] Home Office might deny my immigration, since it would have to assume that I am lying, because my previous petitions were in regard to medical study and a petition for gardener does not fit the picture."

On September 27, Papa wrote Mutti:

> I have to tell you that the children are feeling good and that they are so busy with their schoolwork and playtime that they don't even miss their sweet mom. Hansi asked me casually for the first time when mom is coming back again. He is already excited about going to school the next day and seems to be very happy at school. Luckily there is a boy nearby, who is in the third grade. He speaks some German and looks after Hansi a good deal. He lives very close to us and came by to pick up Hansi at seven thirty this morning. Then the four of us — Lisl also wanted to come to school — went on our way. At noon, the kids come home together, so I don't even have to pick up the boy. Yesterday Hansi got an 'A' and today already has two. He is very proud of his achievements. He did his homework right after lunch and now he is working on his own garden in a little plot that Mama staked out

for him. The prospects of a peaceful solution, especially regarding Hungary, seem to be getting better day by day. Let's hope for the best.

At the end, he wrote, "I hope you won't have any more troubles and that you will be able to tell me the date of your arrival, soon. ... I am thinking of you. ... And I am much calmer about the future, though I must admit, I have no good reason, yet. ... I am sending you a thousand sweet kisses, Arthur."

The next day, my father wrote, "The children and I are continuing to do well. Hansi has already done his homework and he got an 'A' again today. We are all sleeping together in the double bed and we get up shortly after six A.M."

Moving to England seemed like a real possibility and Mutti continued to explore it. "I was at the Society of Friends twice," she wrote. "Our file is being handled but it will take a while. This time I went there specifically to get addresses of Scottish monasteries and hospitals. I wanted to write to the monasteries for [a job for] me and to the hospitals for [a job for] you. Maybe I'll send an ad to the dentist in Edinburgh. I'll send you the directory of English hospitals which the Friends gave me." She closed with an endearment, "I'm sending you thousands of kisses, your old, sweet little wife."

A few days later, indicating how important Papa's letters were to her, she wrote, "It is nine o'clock and I am very tired, but I do have to write you, even though you have been such a bad boy. ... I only received two postcards from you in the last few days."

In a subsequent letter she was back to practical matters, saying, "I just returned from meeting a Dr. Pohl who was a lecturer in London for the past two years. Based on his information, I believe that it should be quite easy for me to find a job in Edinburgh and I am already thinking of applying. ... They are also intending to make the admissions process easier for physicians to study in England."

By the end of September, Mutti was hopeful of having every-thing wrapped up in a matter of weeks. She wrote, "I have arranged emigration for October 31." She wrestled with the question of when to move out of the apartment. If she moved out, she would have to live in her parents' house and provide her new address to the cen-tral registration office. "I can register in the Landstrasse [where her parents lived]," she wrote to Papa. "Or should I keep the apartment ... in order to get a 'key' payment? People have been coming by to look often, but no one has taken it yet."

And So It Continues ...

————————

Ms. Emma Cadbury of the Society of Friends in Vienna wrote Papa on October 22, "We have your letter to Ms. Derenburg and we are sending it to the German Jewish Aid Committee in London. We are suggesting that it may eventually be possible for you to go to India to help in the new health work of the Indian provinces. This may take a while but seems a possible opening for well-qualified doctors."

A representative of the German Jewish Aid Committee wrote, "I had the opportunity of speaking to a Mr. Nehru just before he left England ... and arranged to send out a list of good Austrian and German doctors who would be suitable for practice among the native populations in the provinces there. He stressed the necessity for such doctors taking on this work in the knowledge that they must adapt themselves to native conditions in the sense that they cannot expect to be paid at the high rates existing in the Indian medical service." So India appeared on the screen. But eventually that possibility, like many others, faded away.

India was not the only exotic location that arose as a possible destination. Papa commented, "The climate in Baghdad will make it hard because of the heat. England has a lot of fog, India has many snakes and Palestine too many Arabs."

On October 24, Papa's contact in Canada, Mr. Heller, wrote, "I have tried through every channel to obtain an entrance visa for you and three weeks ago while at Ottawa I was assured that not only your case, but that of a large group of Jewish people, would receive a special permit. One week later I was informed by telegram from a good friend of mine, engaged in politics, and working on your case, that this order had been cancelled." He promised to keep working on our behalf, but the Canadian commissioner of immigration wrote to him, "The Department has every sympathy with these people but unfortunately any relaxation of the regulations would mean the entry of a very large number of them who could not readily be absorbed in the economic structure of this country." That marked the end of the effort to enter Canada.

A few days later, Mutti wrote to Papa:

> At 7:15 A.M., the moving company arrived. Seven men came and they worked like beavers. They were early but we were completely packed. ... The woman down the street came by with her architect and they negotiated me down to 100 marks for the armoire in the entrance hall. They also wanted to buy the bathroom heater but I think I can get more from my brother. Our neighbor, the dentist, came by and bought the door with the sound proofing.
>
> In the afternoon I went back to the income tax office; I had almost forgotten the income tax issue. I would have had to file again. There are new, tougher regulations in effect now. But I was able to settle it on the second visit. Then I went to the savings bank. There we had a problem because I did not have a check signed by you. But the man in charge was very helpful and he submitted all my papers to the exchange control office. There it's going to a section where I know the clerk well. I'll go there in

two days. No use going earlier.

Then I went to get an estimate for the transportation costs so I can submit that to the exchange control office. Then I went to the restaurant because I had no cash left.

After a bit of gossip, it was back to business: "Do you think I can buy my ship passage here to America or wherever else we go?"

She asked Papa about selling a painting to raise enough cash for the moving company, and ended, "My dear Arthur, I miss all of you very much. I hope I will have accomplished everything soon. ... Many, many sweet kisses, your Resa."

Papa replied on November 2, "Don't buy ship tickets yet; we don't know where we are going." And then, "Do you have an idea when you'll be able to find your way home to your husband? I am not incredibly anxious but I would really like to know. ... Kisses to the sweet parents and the siblings. I am sending you a thousand kisses, your old Arthur."

With the furniture packed and stored, Mutti was poised to move on. The next letter read:

It is five o'clock in the morning. I am just waking up. Finally, I have a little bit of quiet. I was running around like a chicken with its head cut off. There was not enough time to run that many errands, but I really want to come and see all of you.

Dearest sweetheart, I was not as sad about the apartment as I had thought. When I closed the door behind the movers and read your sign for the thousandth time, I had a feeling of great gratitude for all the good things I got to experience there and I thanked you in my heart for all the love

we share. ... I'll be arriving on Sunday with the early
train, if I get the tax clearance by then. It would be nice
to get everything taken care of. Many kisses, your
old wife.

With the apartment closed, Mutti would return to her parents'
house and restaurant at the end of her day chasing permits. It was
another world — a world of people going about their business as
they had before, people under no duress from the Nazis. As an Aryan, Mutti moved comfortably in that world as usual. But now she
also had a foot in another world — one of the people under enormous pressure to escape. She found it hard to shake off the sense of
frenzied urgency of those with whom she had stood in endless lines
day after day for some invaluable slip of paper.

It was so difficult. There were many administrative hurdles,
none more burdensome than "Prinz-Eugen-Strasse," where would-
be emigrants were interviewed. Queues were so long that people
arrived the night before to be sure of getting in.

Author Edmund de Waal writes in *The Hare with Amber Eyes,*
"This office will show that it is possible to go in with your wealth
and citizenship and depart a few hours later with only a permit to
leave. People are becoming the shadow of their documents. They
are waiting for their papers to be validated, waiting for letters of
support from overseas, waiting for promises of a position. People
who are already out of the country are begged for favors, for money,
for evidence of kinship, for chimerical ventures, for anything written on any headed paper at all."

Mutti could not bring herself to use the name "Central Office
for Jewish Emigration." She simply referred to it as "going to Prinz-
Eugen-Strasse."

Letters continued to flow back and forth. To Mrs. Bruce in
England, who had generously offered to host our family in Eng-

land, Papa wrote back on November 5, "Thank you for your kind invitation. Unfortunately I still don't know when I can come to England because as yet I have not gotten a permit. I shall come alone to England and my wife and the children will remain here [in Hungary] with my mother. The financial aids I would receive in England are not high enough to allow me to bring my whole family, as I have to stay there for more than a year until I will have received my registration in Edinburgh."

On November 28, Ms. Derenburg of the German Jewish Aid Committee in London wrote, "Mrs. Bruce and other friends of yours over here have been in touch with us in connection with the permit we hope to obtain for you from the Home Office here to study for a British degree with a view to eventually establishing yourself in Kenya."

Possible emigration to the United States required a specific job offer. On November 3, Father Joseph Ostermann, the executive director of the Committee for Catholic Refugees from Germany, wrote Papa, "Our Committee has been singularly successful in securing positions for doctors." Unfortunately, Father Ostermann added, "the condition is that they be in the United States. It is for this reason that we are concentrating our efforts in securing an affidavit for you." He and his team continued to work diligently to find someone willing to give an affidavit of support for someone essentially unknown. They did find such a generous soul, a Mister Scott of Los Angeles, who did, in time, provide an affidavit. But a job offer had still not materialized.

Kristallnacht

On November 7, a young man in Paris, a Jew upset about the expulsion of his parents from Poland, shot and killed a German diplomat in Paris. Hitler's reaction was swift. Groups of destructive hooligans, sometimes salted with SS men, ran rampant in Germany. Fires were set to Jewish shops and synagogues. Books and Bibles were thrown in heaps and burned. The night of November 9-10 became known as *"Kristallnacht"* ("Night of Broken Glass") because so many windows were shattered and so many shards of glass lay on the streets. Thirty thousand Jews, mostly young men, were arrested and shipped to concentration camps. Author Martin Gilbert writes, "This twentieth century pogrom was as violent and far-ranging as any perpetrated in Tsarist Russia half a century earlier."

In Vienna, as part of the Kristallnacht destruction, twenty-two large synagogues and eighty small houses of prayer were blown up or set on fire, and 7,800 Jews were arrested. Over 4,000 Jewish businesses were closed down and 1,900 buildings confiscated. Jews who were still living in their flats were required to turn them over, with no time to pack. The sudden eviction left Jews standing, bewildered, outside their former homes and then desperately looking for a roof somewhere to put over their heads. As historian Giles MacDonogh describes it, "Their remaining valuables were predictably stolen. It provided another chance for informal plunder, and the police had to step in again to dampen the ardor of the Viennese Gentiles."

Edmund de Waal gives stark statistics in *The Hare with Amber Eyes*: "Kristallnacht is a night of terror: 680 Jews commit suicide in Vienna: Twenty-seven are murdered." Incredibly, the Nazis decided that the Jews should be made to pay for the damage and assessed a 1-billion-mark fine on the Jewish community. It was to be paid through a Jewish asset payment (*Judenvermogenagbage*) equal to 20 percent of their assets [MacDonogh].

Kristallnacht marked a critical expansion in the Nazi anti-Jewish efforts, which now expanded from economic pillaging to bodily harm. Physical abuse of Jews had been perpetrated mostly by hooligans, but now it seemed to become state-sponsored. Some experts see Kristallnacht as the beginning of the Holocaust, the mass slaughter of the Jews.

Mutti's efforts to obtain the necessary permits gained urgency, even as they continued to be frustrating. "In the late morning, I was turned down by the Exchange Control Office, despite an appraisal from a respected authority of the medical equipment we want to bring with us. They want a new appraisal report." She ended, "Dear sweetheart, I am exhausted today. I was so incredibly excited about your letter. You have become quite an optimist. Many sweet kisses, your Bunny."

It was already well into November and Papa was increasingly conscious of the approaching expiration of his permit to remain in Hungary.

Brazil

Then, in mid-November, an unexpected breakthrough occurred. Papa received news from a priest in Holland that he had been granted a visa to go to Brazil. Papa confirmed the news with the Brazilian Consulate in Budapest, learning that it was a tourist visa.

The visa came as a result of the letter of recommendation from Cardinal Innitzer of Vienna obtained in May, along with the efforts of the Committee to Assist Persecuted Catholics (Socorro Aos Catolicos Perseguidos) in Rio de Janeiro. We learn this from a letter Papa wrote to Princess Alliata di Montereale living in Palermo, Italy. The princess had given a mutual friend the address of her niece in São Paulo, Brazil. Papa wrote to thank her and described how the visa had been obtained.

Brazil had not appeared earlier in my parents' correspondence and just who orchestrated this complex but successful effort, I do not know. Clearly there was an international network of Catholics helping those wishing to escape the Nazis. The Catholic angle may have succeeded because there were far fewer Catholics trying to escape the Nazis than Jews.

A letter from Papa tells us that a Count Arroyski was involved in the Catholic effort to obtain the visa to Brazil, because Papa promptly wrote to the count thanking him. We do not know how the count became involved and whether he personally knew our family. He may simply have been another of the generous people who were doing what they could in the circumstances to help strangers.

Papa also asked the count two questions. First, did the visa require that he travel to Brazil alone, or could he bring his wife and children with him? The second question involved probing a potentially difficult issue. Without challenging the count, who had after all brought about what was so unexpected and valuable a gift, he needed to know about his ability to work in Brazil. He wrote that he had been told by the Brazilian Consulate in Budapest that the tourist visa would not allow him to practice medicine. That limitation, if not possible to change, made this unexpected opportunity almost unacceptable. It tells us something about the enormous pressure my father was under that he would consider accepting this opportunity even if it meant that he could not practice medicine. Papa knew that no matter where he went, he would most likely have to qualify anew to practice medicine. Still, he always expected eventually to be able to practice. The window for remaining in Hungary was closing; if it was possible to find some country that would allow Papa to earn a living, it needed to happen soon, or we would go to Brazil.

The fact that the news of the visa to Brazil came from Holland had long intrigued me. Mutti had told me as a child that a famous ancestor of her family had lived in Holland. She said his name was Ajax Metzger and that there was a statue in Holland honoring him. In 2006, at a family reunion in Vienna, I heard a more colorful story. Two of my cousins described detailed research that one of our uncles had done years earlier about the ancestor.

The story centers on a lawsuit filed in the early 1800s and carried on for ten years by a great-great-grandfather of ours in Vienna. The lawsuit was against the government of Holland and alleged that our ancestor, named Theobald Metzger von Weibnom, had deposited money with the government (an amount in excess of 100 million guilders) that the government was wrongfully withholding. The Viennese newspapers loved the story and reported on the lawsuit over the years.

Theobald Metzger had served in the Dutch army, where his military skill and bravery led to promotion to general lieutenant of the cavalry. He eventually became the mayor of the city of Breda and served there for ten years. During his life, he acquired several large estates and substantial financial wealth. He died in 1691. Here stories diverge. In the Metzger family version, the government claimed that Theobald had been a pirate and thus his wealth had been forfeited to the Crown; on this basis, the family's claim to his money was denied. The Metzgers accept that Theobald might have been in the Dutch West Indies as a privateer — someone commissioned by the government to harass enemy vessels. They deny that he was anything but a faithful servant of his king.

A less colorful version found in other histories is that Theobald died in Holland in the good graces of the king. The king then had one of his nobles determine if there were heirs. Those histories report that, remarkably, no heirs were found and Theobald's assets were given to someone close to the king. This version notes that there was a war going on and the king needed money. Those histories also mention that there were numerous other claimants and that the Dutch Supreme Council denied all claims on January 21, 1842, ruling that the statute of limitations had run out.

While Papa awaited a response from Count Arroyski about the possibility of practicing medicine in Brazil, Mutti continued her efforts in Vienna to obtain the departure permits and to bring with us Papa's medical equipment. It was now December, well past the October date she had set earlier as an emigration date. And she was aware that Papa's efforts to extend his residence permit in Hungary had been unsuccessful. She was acutely aware of the increasingly tight time pressure.

For Jews in Vienna, it was a dreadful time. Toward the end of the year the Gestapo estimated that they had shipped over 20,000 Austrians to concentration camps since March 16. Three thousand of those died during the winter [MacDonogh].

That was terrible enough, but what the future held was unimaginable. The state was characterizing Jews as traitors to the nation; it was describing them as despoilers of the Aryan race and it was systematically dehumanizing them. Eventually those actions led to what the Nazis called the "Final Solution" — the horrific murder of Jews on an industrialized basis. Today we know that over 6 million Jews were eventually killed by the Nazis in what came to be known as the Holocaust.

Christmas Season in Vienna

A s the year-end holidays approached, my parents decided that Lisl and I would return to Vienna to be with Mutti and spend some time with Omama and Opapa. It must have been Uncle Pista, the husband of Papa's sister Boeszi (Elizabeth), who brought us. It was fun to be back in familiar Vienna after three months in Hungary. Omama and Opapa gave us special long hugs and Mutti was near tears as she held us. The Christmas season had brought out the lights and decorations that made Vienna especially festive. Of course Lisl and I had no idea of the pressure and tension that Mutti was under. We just enjoyed seeing the shop windows, the Christmas trees and the lights. We were staying with Mutti at Omama's house. Mutti told us that she had closed our apartment. That was a surprise, but staying at Omama's was itself an adventure. And Tante Rieda brought over Huber Hansi and we enjoyed playing in the large empty room.

While we played, Mutti was continuing her efforts at the various offices, in particular her nemesis, the office at Prinz-Eugen-Strasse.

On December 7, she wrote to Papa, "I arrived at 6:30 in the morning at Prinz-Eugen-Strasse and waited outside until 8:30. Then I waited inside until 10:15, and got nowhere again. This time they asked for a confirmation of change of address issued by the Central Registration Office. My request for a pass was granted, so I won't have to stand in line and wait out in the street again. Unfortunately they had kept the documents from the City Hall and from the City Council."

Two days later, she wrote again about Prinz-Eugen-Strasse:

> Today I was really distraught. You can imagine why. Whenever I do something stupid — and today I did lots of stupid things — I was taking care of the tax clearance issue, all proud and happy with the pass in my hand. After a few snide comments from the clerk, I was cleared and sent to the second desk. I went straight to the desk labeled 'tax clearance.' There they asked me for the notice from City Hall. That notice, however, had not been returned. The clerk sent me to another man who checked to see if City Hall had received the file and whether City Hall had answered that everything checked out. He could not confirm that, so he said it would be best if I go to City Hall myself and then deliver the response personally. That would speed things up. I tried to get another pass for when I returned but was not able to get one. I was depressed about having to get back at the end of the line when I return.
>
> The income tax office wanted a further payment for the current quarter. I told them you didn't owe anything but they insisted on a prepayment anyway. I also have to give them a declaration of personal assets and list everything we had owned and account for what had been spent. After that is done, they will be able to complete the file right away. Dear Bunny, I really felt like crying today. ... Should I not have paid the tax? I think there is nothing that says I shouldn't have, is there?

Papa quickly answered on December 12. "I beg you, don't make life so hard by blaming yourself. Remember how things went concerning Baghdad," he said, in another reference to the elusive possibility of an escape to Baghdad. He added, "[Remember] how angry you were and how we can laugh about it. It will be the same thing with the tax payment certificate. In retrospect we'll laugh about it too. Not everything works out the first time, but eventually it does."

The next day Papa wrote, "Good news, the Hungarian national bank gave me permission to pay for the ship ticket in *Pengo* [Hungarian currency]." He added, "Today I received my first reply from Rio. It was from the brother of my friend Ina. He believes we should come immediately. He thinks I could open my own practice right away in the southern state of Rio Grande do Sul. In any case, we'll meet more acquaintances there than one thinks. ... It's good to know that we won't be completely among strangers after all."

Mutti, on the other hand, was in despair.

> I wish everything would already be over. And then I treated Mama horribly today. I was so upset when I got home and I said, 'My God I did something stupid today' and Mama immediately replied, 'So what stupid thing did you do this time? I don't understand you. I always think about what I'll do and consider the consequences and then these things don't happen to me!'
>
> Of course, I got angry. That's no way to treat someone who is already distraught. But I realize that she is in a difficult situation right now. She does not get along with Mitzi and that's a big problem. Mitzi had the storage room cleaned up in her absence. It had been neglected and now Mama feels embarrassed and is crying all the time. It is very

difficult. The best thing might be if she were to give up running the business, but that would be a great sacrifice. My dear Bunny, if only I had the tax clearance already, I would feel much more relieved.

I am sending you thousands of kisses. The children are doing well. Love, your old Bunny.

Papa moved to calm the waters. He wrote, "Don't let other people drive you crazy and first and foremost don't blame yourself. You are still my dearest and smartest little wife, who deserves a thousand hugs."

On December 11, Mutti wrote:

I didn't sleep well at all today and I am quite exhausted. In the morning I went to the tax office to get a receipt for the payment and to hand in the list of assets. I have to send another one directly to the finance office. When I was there the clerk told me that he would be readily able to issue an extension of my clearance. That was news to me because the last time I had a very difficult time. However, you are not getting a clearance because a new law has been passed that requires people who have emigrated but still have assets in the country to be specifically registered (astonishing since no new law has in fact been promulgated).

The whole file is now being returned to the tax office in Berlin. ... I asked Spigl [my parents' financial advisor] how we can expedite the processing in Berlin or if there isn't a way to export the crate [with my father's medical instruments] with the old clearance since that clearance had been issued

by the Exchange Control Office itself. He thought
it could and called the Exchange Control Office.
The clerk told him that he thought that would work
but that it would be best to check with the shipping
agent who knows what works in practice. The shipping agent thought it would be difficult but possible. I have to go to the Central Registration Office
to pick up a confirmation of change of address for
him. Then the agent said he'd try it.

On December 12, she wrote: "I stood in line again at 6:45 in
the morning. Mr. Spigl stood faithfully at my side. As a result, we
got special permission to come in. I was able to get through all the
desks until the next to the last one. There I asked that they put the
tax clearance request into my file."

Mutti's older sister, Rieda, had gone to Prinz-Eugen-Strasse to
move Mutti's documents along. Rieda was married to a high-rank-
ing civil servant, the top bureaucrat in the Ministry of Transportation, reporting directly to the Minister of Transportation. She was
also a large woman with an air of self-confidence. One can imagine
that she did not enter the office hat in hand, deferentially, like other
petitioners. More likely she strode in like a confident citizen expecting prompt service from bureaucrats. Instead the bureaucrats
at Prinz-Eugen-Strasse threw her out. That tells you that even good
Aryan citizens had little standing at Prinz-Eugen-Strasse.

Mutti wrote, "They were very proud at the income tax office
that they were the first to process cases under the new law which
requires that files be sent back to Berlin. The clerk also told me that
they had sent my file back to Prinz-Eugen-Strasse. Now they will
either send it to Berlin or destroy it. In any case, I would like to
retrieve the file and send it to the tax office in Berlin myself since I
saw at the travel agency so many people who cannot leave simply

because they can't get back documents that had already been processed by the tax office."

Woven throughout all of Mutti's efforts was the support of her
family. Mutti's brother Fonsus (Alfons) often lent his assistance. He
was effective, had good judgment and both my parents relied on
him. Alfons volunteered in his direct and forceful way to help with
the tax documents. On December 16, Mutti wrote, "If the file really needs to go to Berlin, Fonsus will drive with me there and he
will tell them that he will cover any charges we might incur and we
hope that we'll be able to take care of the matter that way, assuming
that the file, when it was returned to Prinz-Eugen-Strasse, wasn't
just tossed in the garbage as something that cannot be processed.
It was such bad luck that Fonsus had to leave right now. That cost
us critical days, but I sincerely hope that they did not throw it away
so quickly."

Five days before Christmas, as time was getting very short to
meet the deadline for Papa to leave Hungary, there was another
scare in Vienna. Mutti wrote anxiously, "My file was misplaced and
I had given up hope that it would be found. I had planned to start
all over again. In the end the file was found and I was promised that
I would have it in my hands in three days."

"Please, sweetheart," she continued, "cross your fingers that the
file at least will not get lost again and that I don't have to start all
over." She ended, "I am sending you thousands of kisses. Our Lisl
has a terrible cold again. Love, your old, sweet wife."

As winter settled in, it got very cold. Mutti told us later that
she often put newspapers in her shoes as insulation in the hope of
keeping her feet warm. Those were the days before high-tech boots.
Hers were made of simple unlined leather and the cold came right
through when she stood in the cold for hours.

About that time Mutti received another letter from Ruth Mellanby in London, who had written earlier about a gardening pro-

gram. The letter, dated December 11, said, "Last week, I received from Mr. Loy a sworn statement about his intentions of setting you up in a practice in Nairobi. I took it immediately to the medical committee at Woburn house from where it was sent to the Home Office. ... I am hoping to write you in the course of the next week or two and tell you that your application to live and study here has been granted."

My father had finally managed to get an extension on his permit to remain in Hungary. It was to have expired in mid-December; the extension was until January 5. However, the authorities said that if he overstayed his permit, they would send him back to Vienna. Papa had some difficulty understanding why the Hungarian authorities were putting so many stumbling blocks in his way. He was a native of Hungary and had served with distinction in the army. Was it that he had moved to Austria and taken Austrian citizenship? It was probably not his Jewish origin because Jews in Hungary, unlike in Austria, were treated as equal citizens. Whatever it was, he thought he had to take seriously their threat to eject him to Austria.

He wrote to the British Home Office in London with some desperation to ask the status of his permit to enter and do a medical residence there. But more and more, it looked like we were going to Brazil.

Mutti was also very conscious of all that remained to be done as Christmas approached. "I will be seeing you soon and I miss you terribly, but I really don't want to miss anything and so it is possible that I'll only come over the holidays or in the worst case will bring the kids to you in Gyor [a Hungarian city about halfway between Vienna and Budapest]. My dearest Bunny, all the hard stuff is only temporary and I hope that maybe everything will turn out well in the end."

On December 20, the strain of repeated disappointments and

postponements was wearing on Papa as he faced a last hurdle to go to Brazil in getting a visa to pass through Yugoslavia en route to the embarkation port in Trieste, Italy. He worried about what might await in Brazil. Papa wrote, "I am starting to get nervous now; it's just a short time before the departure. Everything — except for the Yugoslavian visa — has actually been taken care of and now I am slowly starting to worry about Brazil. Today an answer arrived from the Santa Catharina rehabilitation center in São Paulo, Brazil. They are sorry, they don't have a position for me." On a lighter note, he added, "Mama was so happy to get the note from Hansi."

Two days later, he wrote, "My Yugoslavian visa will take about one more week and then I will actually be ready to travel."

Since Christmas was only days away, gifts for family members became a topic of correspondence, and a relief from tales of difficulty. Mutti wrote, "I tried on my dress today and I hope you'll like it. I would like to give Mimi [my father's niece] my ski equipment for Christmas. I think she'll really enjoy that. For Mama, I have the fabric 'you got' (didn't I put that nicely) or whatever else you think and for Boeszi [my father's sister] I have lots of ideas. I'll have to see how the money situation is looking. I would love to have everything that a 'lady' needs for putting on make-up etc. since I heard that the women in Rio are very fashionable and I want to change myself. Please, I am serious." Papa replied promptly to Mutti's remark that she wanted to change herself. "I am vehemently opposed to you wanting to change yourself. Please stay the way you are, just not where you are."

Then Papa passed along a request from his mother, "Mama asked me that you should buy a small book for her to learn Portuguese. She said she knows very well that she'll never be able to come visit us but it comforts her nevertheless when she can speak some Portuguese."

Christmas brought other questions. Mutti wrote, inquiring,

"Dearest sweetheart, I would like to ask you whether the 24th is very important to your mother or if she would be fine with celebrating Christmas on the 25th. My mother is very easy going and understanding but I think I won't be able to get away from here soon. Maybe I'll only come to visit you with the children over the holidays and then leave them there so I can come right back and take care of whatever I can. In any case, I want to keep on fighting until the last minute. The stakes are high and, after all, you should be able to work."

Papa responded. "I hope ... that you will be able to rest at least between Christmas and departure. Your coming here is affecting so many. I, Mama and all the others would be very sad if you won't be here for Christmas Eve. Bear in mind that it would be perhaps the last time that Mama will be able to have the children at her place. Please be here for Christmas Eve."

Mutti had another question. "Mama wants to give me her two exquisite opal earrings for Christmas. Is that alright with you?"

Papa thought it was too much. "Tell your sweet mother thank you for wanting to give up her earrings. However, I think it is too much of a sacrifice and we won't be able to benefit much from it. What about that nice old necklace? Is it made of gold? If so, ask for that instead." He must have been thinking of the likely need to sell or pawn the jewelry.

Mama's letter continued, "We are very sad around here. Mama is crying her eyes out. She can't give up the business and Mitzi and Alfons want her out. You can imagine what kind of constant conflicts and agitation this causes. I am sure that it is a very hard time for her and as an outsider it is easy to see the mistakes others are making but I am not able to help them." Mama may have been crying her eyes out at the prospect of losing our family.

She continued, describing the generosity of her four brothers, "Fritz gave me a beautiful book about South America. People keep giving me things. Yesterday Toni gave me 40 Reichmarks and said he would bring me more. Josi offered me his savings bank book and told me to take what I needed and Fonsus wants to provide whatever guarantees we need. We can't complain about our relatives."

On December 22, the local British Passport Office in Vienna responded to my father's inquiry about the status of the permit to enter England. They stated, "It is noted that a guarantee for you and your family has been registered with the Home Office, London." As he read that, Papa must have thought, God bless Bruce and Ellis and Loy; they are doing what they promised. Unfortunately, as Papa read further he saw the terribly disappointing news, "We beg to inform you that up to the present, no authority has been received from London to grant you visas."

Papa was in a terrible bind. It was December 23. The Christmas and year-end holidays had begun; it was most unlikely that the British Home Office would grant him a visa before some time in January. His residence permit would expire on January 5 and he had come to believe that he could not risk overstaying his permit in Hungary. Papa made the difficult decision to take what he had in hand, the visa to enter Brazil, despite its critical limitation prohibiting him from practicing medicine. He decided that he had no option for the family but to leave for Brazil.

Time Runs Out

O n December 30, my father wrote Mrs. Mellanby in London: "Thank you for all your help and for delivering the letter from Mr. Loy to the Society of Friends. Regrettably, I have to inform you that since I can no longer remain in Hungary, and since we now have a visa to enter Brazil, we will have to leave for Brazil in early January. I will make a trial in Brazil and should it prove to be a failure, I hope to obtain a British permit and start my studies in Edinburgh as soon as I receive permission from the University to do so. The latest news from the University is not very reassuring because they indicate that I would not be able to commence my studies before October 1940" — almost two years in the future.

Mutti received the necessary tax clearance on December 23 and

The hard-won tax clearance certificate.

she, Lisl and I all made it to Hungary for Christmas. She brought a letter from Opapa to Papa. It read, "All of us send you warm Christmas greetings. Enjoy each other's happy company. Now, you are able to be truly happy and can celebrate this beautiful Christmas with cheer. Resa had to go through quite a bit, but thank God, it's all over and it ended well. Basically, it was a continuous struggle, but with a happy end. Resa will need a few days of great rest because it was too much for the poor thing. Thursday or maybe already Wednesday she has to go back to Vienna! I hope you are doing well! We are also doing well! We are wishing you, Resa, and the dear children a very good and happy journey and also a blessed New Year. Warmest regards and kisses, your loving parents-in-law."

On January 4, 1939, our family boarded an overnight train in Budapest for Trieste, Italy. On the train ride, Mutti had tears in her eyes. "What's the matter, Mutti? Why are you crying?" I asked.

She answered, "I think I have lost a beautiful brooch that Papa gave me. I can't find it anywhere and I loved it very much."

"Well," I said, trying to comfort her, "it was probably just mislaid in all the rush of packing. I'm sure you'll find it again."

"I hope so," she replied, and gave me a long hug.

But, of course, she had many reasons for her tears.

Our family boarded the ocean liner *Neptunia* in Trieste on January 5, 1939. That evening the ship cast off and we began the voyage to a new life in Brazil.

2

A NEW BEGINNING

A NEW BEGINNING

Sailing Away

Austria is a landlocked country and the largest body of water I had ever seen was the Danube River. The first morning at sea, Papa took Lisl and me out on the deck. Although we could glimpse land off one side, the dark blue water of the Mediterranean filled our view. It was breathtaking.

The ship sailed quietly along; birds flew overhead, and sometimes we saw other smaller ships heading in various directions. There was usually land visible but sometimes the Mediterranean Sea stretched to the horizon. It was vastly different from what I had known — the city of Vienna and the Danube or the meadows and mountains of Hungary — but it was awesome, and exciting.

On the third morning, we approached land, and slowed to enter a harbor. Before us an amphitheatre of white buildings rose up, as if from the water. It was the port of Algiers. The clear air and bright sun burnished the buildings, which seemed to sparkle in the light. Vienna's buildings, handsome as they were, were gray. After the ship docked, we disembarked and walked through the narrow, shadowed streets of the old quarter of Algiers. There were donkeys in the street and men and women wearing what looked like long, heavy dresses. Everything was new — it was a fascinating revelation.

We sailed off that evening. When I woke the next day, we were out of sight of land; the quiet ocean stretched endlessly in all directions. The motion of the ship felt soothing; it was almost

Lisl and Mutti on the ship to Brazil.

hypnotic to watch the ship cut through the water, tossing white-capped waves to either side.

Our family shared a stateroom. That itself was a playful change from a large apartment; it was an adventure, and enjoyable, since it was not going to be for a long time. We ate every meal in what was like a restaurant and that, too, was fun. Still, I think we all were looking forward to seeing land and arriving at our destination.

My parents enjoyed going on deck, sitting in the deck chairs and chatting with other passengers. They met one young man who might have been distantly related to us: his last name, Holz-meister, was similar to the maiden name of Grandma Paula, my Hungarian grandmother — Holzmann. In any event, he became a good friend and our family saw him, and eventually his Brazilian wife, years later in the U.S. where they lived for a while in my parents' summer cottage.

At Last, Brazil

After a week at sea, we finally saw land: Brazil. We stood by the rail in anticipation as we entered Bahia, the ship's first port of call.

While Algiers was serene and white, my dominant memory of Bahia is bustle and bright color. Our ship tied up in a cluster of busy docks, with smaller vessels all around us and men everywhere cleaning fishing boats or moving large sacks on dollies. There was activity in all directions. Some of the men working on the docks and on the boats were black, something else to look at and absorb. I had never seen a Negro in Vienna or in Hungary.

Beyond the docks, rising from the harbor, a large, tower-like structure stood some six stories high. That, we were told, was the elevator to the city, which stood on a bluff overlooking the harbor. Soon we were riding up the windowless lift. When we stepped out, the sun was as bright as Algiers, but the air was heavier and more humid. There was also a stunning array of large, colorful flowers.

Bahia, we were told, had 365 churches — one for every day of the year. We visited a memorable one. Hanging from the ceiling along the high walls were a large number of crutches, canes and plaster casts of arms, legs and torsos. Each, we learned, was a gift of thanks for the cure of the limb or body part on display. It was a catalog of miracles. I believed it and was happy to be in so remarkable a place.

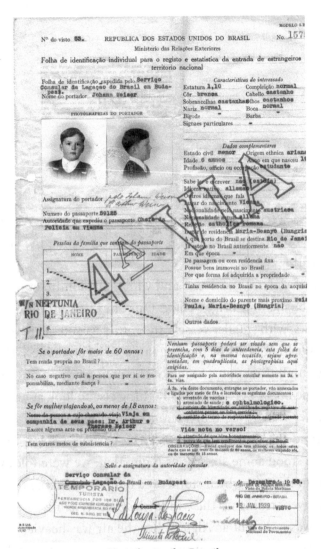

Hansi's visa for Brazil.

We returned to the ship and headed out to sea. On the second morning, as we approached Rio, our final destination, everyone was on deck. The mountains around the city came into view and we sailed past the islands that mark the harbor. Then the city itself appeared — the handsome residential areas and their glorious beaches. The ship sailed by the landmark Sugar Loaf Mountain and into the huge lagoon behind the residential sections where the harbor and the industrial areas lie.

We disembarked, said goodbye to the crew and waited for our luggage to be unloaded. The luggage came and we waited some more. Other passengers moved on and waved goodbye; soon we were the only ones left at the dock. Large black women in long dresses swept the dock with straw brooms. Finally, a small man wearing leather gloves came up to us and introduced himself as Mr. Baum from the Committee to Assist Persecuted Catholics (Socorro Aos Catolicos Perseguidos), the group that had promised to help us. He led us to a waiting taxi and off we went.

The Committee to Assist Persecuted Catholics (Socorro Aos Catolicos Perseguidos) in Rio provided support for Papa.

The taxi darted through the traffic. We were so busy holding on that we could barely watch the passing scene. We rode beyond the large cranes near the big ships and moved toward the city proper with its tall buildings, higher than what I was used to in Vienna. We went to the office of the head of the committee, who was out for the moment. While we waited, I moved to an open window and looked down at the street. I could barely take it all in. There was a lot of hubbub and to me, confusion. The street was full of people, hawking goods, shouting to each other, singing, walking not just on the sidewalk but also in the street alongside carts, bicycles and more cars. There was bright sun and lots of color. It was so different from what I knew and loved in Vienna, where around the stately buildings — the theater, museum, parliament, city hall — and the orderly, trim cityscape, people moved and spoke quietly, politely. Rio's kaleidoscope of colors and sounds just seemed so different.

The Count

Then the head of the committee arrived. Count Morazevsky was a tall man, well dressed. He had a warm smile, greeted my parents like friends, and tousled my hair. He welcomed us and said we would be guests of the committee for the time being.

Papa expressed his hope that the committee might find him some work, in a clinic or laboratory. The count sympathetically explained that there were serious difficulties. Papa's tourist visa limited his right to work. But beyond that, it would be practically impossible for him to get a license as a doctor. Doctors in Brazil were required to have had five years of Brazilian schooling and to have served in the armed forces. Papa looked dejected. The seriousness of his professional plight was just beginning to sink in.

Mutti jumped in, "Both my husband and I would really like to start working as soon as possible." Mr. Baum pointed out that often women found it easier to find work and suggested sending Mutti to a smaller nearby city where she might have a better opportunity to find an office position while Papa stayed home with the children. He also thought it might be good to send me away to school.

Mutti could hardly restrain herself. "Oh, please, don't think of splitting us up. We have lost everything, except for the four of us. Nothing is more important for us than to be together and to support each other. We will find a way out of this, but please do not separate us."

The count promised to work to keep the family together, then sent us off with Mr. Baum.

As we rode in another taxi, we observed again how different Rio was from Vienna. All the windows, even on the trolleys, were open. Many shops were open to the street with shelves extending over the threshold. Vienna had an air of stability and order. Here it seemed that nothing stood still. And it was hot.

New Homes

The taxi turned into a narrow street that threaded its way up a hill. We bumped along cobblestones and swerved to avoid potholes. The street was flanked by stone houses whose flaking paint and broken stucco were camouflaged by large bougainvillea bushes with red, purple or pink flowers. They gave an air of glamour to houses otherwise down at the heels. Mr. Baum introduced us to an older, short, stocky, dark-haired woman wearing a loose, slightly soiled housedress and smoking a cigarette. He said goodbye and left quickly.

The landlady showed us into a large second-floor room that seemed cramped with a couch, a double bed, a large crib, and a chest of drawers. On a chair was a basin and jug. The landlady nodded toward the jug and said, "That's all the water you'll have today. We are on short rations." Our several trunks took up most of the remaining space in the room. The landlady turned to leave, saying, "Dinner will be at six o'clock."

Papa waited a few moments and then turned to Mutti and said, "Go down the hall and find the bathroom. If there's a tub we might sneak in a quick bath for the kids."

Mutti walked carefully down the hall, found the bathroom and came back. Then she told Lisl and me to be very quiet, took us to the bathroom, and stripped off our clothes. She slowly filled the tub. The water was brown at first but soon cleared, and she put us in. Then she decided to throw our underwear in as well. She kept making eyes at us to remind us to be quiet. I whispered, "Is it wrong to take a bath?"

"It may be more water than we are supposed to have today but it's even more wrong to leave you so dirty," she replied. "So we are doing the lesser wrong." I nodded as though I understood.

Papa poked his head in and said not to let the water out until we went to dinner. He said that when everybody was eating, they might not hear the water draining out.

At six o'clock, Mutti took Lisl and me to the dining room. It was dominated by a large table covered by an oilcloth, with a dozen chairs around it. We soon met the half dozen other residents — two girls who were members of the chorus in a musical, two boys who were students, another girl who was an orphan and a young man who was the boyfriend of one of the actresses. Mutti referred to him as a "street lawyer." Having begun to study Portuguese only a few weeks earlier, Papa haltingly applied his meager command of the language to chat with the others as we ate. Later he told Mutti of the odd arrangements some of the youngsters had. When the two girls went to work at the theater, the two students would use their beds. When the girls came back, the boys vacated the beds and found some chairs to sleep in until they went off to school.

The cook came out with a big pot of beans and rice and served everyone. Then he brought a platter of thin slices of meat, very tough but tasty. I was hungry enough that I could eat anything — and I did. When it was over, Lisl and I asked about dessert. We were delighted to hear that we would have bananas. Bananas were rare in Austria and we thought it wonderful to be in a place where bananas grew right there. But when the plate with the fruit came out, we were really disappointed. There were two small dark things on the plate that almost looked like sausages. One of the young girls took one, peeled it, showed us that it was white inside and gave it to us. They were actually very sweet bananas. We finished them in no time.

Back in our room, Mutti put me on the couch and Lisl in the crib. Then she told us a story. She was a very good storyteller. We were soon asleep.

The next day, Mutti told us that she and Papa had spent a long time looking out the window at the stars. Maybe it reminded them of looking at the stars from our small balcony in Kuchelau, although here you would be looking at different constellations, including one they called the Southern Cross. Now Lisl and I joined them at the window. We could just see some people moving in the garden behind a wall across the street, perhaps refugees like us. Mutti and Papa decided to go visit them.

A nice European lady seemed almost to be waiting for us at the door. Mrs. Stern was also from Vienna; her husband was a lawyer. In the garden we met two other couples and a former shopkeeper who was alone. In addition, there was Ruth, a girl of about 5, and a baby. At one end of the garden there was a small tree and I began making little stick figures from twigs. Ruth giggled as I described the figures. Lisl, of course, was her sunny self and just enjoyed everything.

As we played, the adults chatted. My parents learned that these people were also guests of the committee, but that they had been there for almost six months and seemed depressed at the difficulty of finding work.

Mutti's manuscript records a conversation between the lawyer and Papa, about the situation of the Jews in Germany and Austria. Papa said, "Maybe we kept our heads in the sand. We did not want to believe what we heard and saw."

"Of course not," the lawyer said. "My uncle and aunt lived in Germany and they could not believe that Hitler was more than a passing phase. One saw it as a rash on a healthy body — a temporary discomfort. The family had lived in Germany for generations; the men had fought for the homeland in the First World War; they were deeply involved in the community. They could not believe that their neighbors would abandon them." He told the story of a Jewish neighbor, a doctor. When a Nazi stood by his front door to direct patients away, the doctor put on his old World War I uniform with the Iron Cross he'd won in battle and stood next to the Nazi. The Nazi fellow eventually left. But it was a short-lived victory; it couldn't hold back the flood. The patients drifted away. The doctor sent his son to an uncle in the United States, then one night he waited for his wife to fall asleep and turned on the gas, taking both of their lives.

There were other stories of German Jews who had remained in Germany, unwilling to believe that the good sense of the Germans would not take charge and bring things back to normal. Most waited too long. Perhaps the Austrians hoped that the Treaty of Versailles would hold and that Germany would not be allowed to annex Austria. Or that Austrians, ever relaxed and fun-loving, would not accept the stern, hard-eyed Germans. Still, the Nazi party had been growing ever stronger in Austria. One hoped that good sense would prevail, but Jews had seen again and again that when some society-wide problem arose, they were too often persecuted for causing it, however absurd the claim.

The former shopkeeper told Papa he could get a license to practice medicine. "The law limiting a foreigner's right to practice was only adopted a few years ago," he said. "So you look at a list of ships that arrived here and pick one that arrived before the law was passed." Papa replied, "That would be dishonest." The man said, "They are not after people like you, who are real doctors. They are after charlatans who only pretend to be doctors." Papa said, "Perhaps, but that's not the way I want to go."

When we got back to our boarding house, Mutti said to Papa,

"We've got to get going. We still have momentum from all the rushing around we did to get out of Europe. I don't want to just sit and wait." And a day or two later, she went to see the count by herself, to try to find work. When she came back, she was glowing with excitement. She gave all of us big hugs and said, "We're going to have a home of our own, right by the ocean. It will be wonderful." The count had told her of a young Brazilian doctor who had come to Rio on his honeymoon and had stopped by to ask for an experienced surgeon who could join him in a new hospital he was setting up in southern Brazil. The young doctor's license would cover Papa. It would be a matter of a week or two, but when the doctor's honeymoon was over, he would be ready to have us head down to join him.

Papa and Mutti enjoyed a long hug. Lisl and I did not understand it all, but I had heard something about a new home and I was very happy. A new home was certainly what I wanted.

The next day we went for a picnic in the park. After a hot walk, we arrived at the park, found a bench and sat down. Now we could look at the trees and flowers and vines around us. They were all so different from what we knew. The trees had branches that stretched far out from the trunk and were supported by something my mother called "air roots." They looked like crutches. And there were vines growing up and into the trees, like they wanted to choke them. It made our pine forests back home look neat by comparison. The flowers were also different — very large and bright. Some seemed the size of dinner plates. And the birds also seemed bigger than life with bright colors and with squawks rather than songs. It was a lot to take in.

As we returned home, we saw some unusual activity. One of the girls said, "Hurry, get your clothes and things together and move them to the house across the street." It turned out that the landlady hadn't paid the rent on the house and we were being evicted.

We moved our trunks across the street, and just then, we began to smell something cooking in the kitchen. The cook was still on the job. All the other tenants seemed to be doing something else, but Mutti, Papa, Lisl and I sat down and ate all the beans and rice the cook dished out, plus more bananas than usual. When we finished, we took a short walk up the street and then returned to our room, lay down and fell asleep.

The next thing I knew, the world was shaking. I was still half asleep; when I opened my eyes I saw a big man rattling the couch I was sleeping on. The man said, "We're taking the furniture and if you don't get up, we'll take you too." Papa got the last trunk out, onto the street. Then he headed toward town. We needed a new place to live.

The refugees across the street invited us in while we waited. I tried to play with the little girl but I kept worrying about where Papa was and where we would go next. It was several hours later before he returned. "We are in luck," he said. "I found a nice place with a garden right outside our window and a good German-Brazilian couple as landlords. I have a taxi outside and a small truck for our trunks."

Our second boarding house was set back from the sidewalk with a small lawn, bordered by flowering plants. Two large windows set low with their sills just above ground level were the windows to our room, which was half below ground level. Mutti said it must have been the storage room because it was full of furniture — armoires, rocking chairs, easy chairs, a big bed, and two smaller ones. There was barely room for our trunks but Mutti rearranged everything and it all fit.

The door to the room was at the back and opened up to an open area where sheets hung on a line, flapping in the wind. Beyond that was a small garden with dill growing along the edge by the building wall.

The next morning, we went upstairs to a large airy room where meals were served. Sunlight was coming in the front windows and we could see out the back to the little garden. The landlady, a warm German woman, made pancakes for Lisl and me. They were not the light fluffy pancakes Mutti used to make, but it was a nice welcoming gesture.

The boarding house was on a main street that ran from the ocean to the Tunnel Novo ("new tunnel"), which connected two parts of Rio separated by a large hill that ran down to the sea. As the key connector between two parts of the city, Avenida Princessa Isabel was a busy road with a trolley line and a steady flow of cars and trucks. There were shops and pedestrians heading in both directions. I liked the activity. There was always something to see. During the day, I often leaned on the windowsill to watch all the activity outside — trolleys full of people, trucks carrying loads that hung over their sides, and a whole range of pedestrians walking by. It was full of life. You could imagine all kinds of stories. Across the street were restaurants, bars and shops, many of which stayed open late into the evening with their lights on. And cars drove by with their headlights on at night. As I lay in bed, I could see all kinds of light patterns on the ceiling.

Mutti continued to look for work, as did Papa. But really, everybody was waiting for the young doctor to come back from his honeymoon so we could move south to a new productive life.

Two weeks later, the count asked my parents to come by his office, and informed them that the plan for the new hospital had been cancelled. "We'll keep our eyes open for other things," he promised.

There was nothing to do but bear the disappointment and continue with what Mutti later described as "the terrible struggle to earn our daily bread." She was getting some materials from the committee to translate from Portuguese into English, French or German, three languages she spoke well. She was still learning Portuguese but knew enough to make sense of what she was asked to translate into the requested language. She had also put out word that she was available to teach piano, but no lessons had yet been booked.

Papa sometimes helped with the translations, but usually he went out every day searching for a clinic or hospital that could use his professional skills. Despite his qualifications and the understanding that he would work assisting a Brazilian doctor, the institutions were not ready to take on an unlicensed doctor. So he would come home, disappointed and tired. Still, the next day, he'd be out again pursuing leads from the count and others of doctors who might be interested in having Papa work with them. The leads were dead ends as well, but Papa saw no choice but to keep searching and hoping that perhaps some crumb would fall from the table.

Letter from London

And then, in late February, a letter from London brought wonderful news. Papa beamed as he read it and Mutti had tears in her eyes. The letter was dated January 17; sent to Papa's address in Hungary, it had taken a month to reach him at his new address, "Care of the Committee to Assist Persecuted Catholics," in Rio de Janeiro.

In the letter, Yvonne Kapp of the Medical Department of the German Jewish Aid Committee in London wrote, "I have much pleasure in informing you that the Home Office have granted permission to come to this country and I want to advise you to get in touch with the British Passport Control Office [in Budapest] mentioning your Home Office Ref. No. W. 10488 in order to obtain your visas."

The long-sought and elusive visa had finally been authorized. All their letter writing and all their telephone calls and all the generous effort of Mr. Bruce and his team had actually paid off.

Papa moved quickly to seize the opportunity, and promptly wrote to the British Passport Control Office in Budapest, "I am obliged to inform you that ... as I had no possibility to remain in Hungary I had to leave for Brazil and I am staying now with my family in Rio de Janeiro. In order to obtain my visa, may I ask you the favor to send as early as possible the permit that the British Home Office granted me to the British Consulate in Rio de Janeiro."

When Papa informed Count Morazevsky of the development, the count was almost as pleased as Papa.

Papa had earlier written Mrs. Bruce and Mr. Ellis that he had been forced to leave for Brazil. Ellis replied, "I had already discovered that you had left for Brazil just before the British permit was granted, and am naturally sorry it should be so, but on the other hand I daresay you appreciate the vast number of candidates with whom the British authorities and the different refugee societies have to deal, and can therefore understand the immensity of their problem. I have written the German Jewish Aid Centre, who were handling your case, advising them of your whereabouts and that you still desire to come to England."

There was nothing more to do now but wait for the British bureaucracy to move slowly to the highly anticipated and expected conclusion. In the meantime, there were mouths to feed and Papa and Mutti continued with "the daily struggle" to put bread on the table. But there was real optimism now.

At the boarding house, our trunks continued to be our closets and wardrobes. We took our clothes out to wear them and put them back when they were washed. But they stayed musty, and more than once Mutti said she yearned to spread them in the sun and air everything out. Once we had an exciting alternative to washing our clothes. We were getting ready to go out; the air felt unusually heavy and damp. Papa looked out and said, "Quick, get some clothes on you want washed. We are going to have a big downpour." Outside, I could see dark gray clouds over the tops of the buildings. Soon there was a huge shaft of lightning, followed by a crack and a roar. We took off our clothes and Mutti soaped them up. We put them back on and ran barefoot out into the yard just as the rain began. It was like standing under a very big shower. Everybody else was running for cover and we were jumping in the rain. Like all heavy storms, it lightened quickly and we came in to take off our wet clothes. We were still laughing as Mutti rubbed us dry.

The visa to England was the big news but efforts that had been underway before continued to bear some fruit. The effort launched by Mrs. Wagner and Miss Rieff had been passed on to Reverend Ostermann and the Committee for Catholic Refugees from Germany. The committee eventually learned that we had moved to Brazil and followed up. Father Ostermann wrote on March 8, "Since you are at the present time in Rio de Janeiro, please send us a listing of the requirements demanded by the authorities in that country for permission to emigrate to the United States."

A month later, on April 11, he notified my father of the results of the committee's hard work, "The immigration affidavit, together with supporting financial documentation made out in your behalf by Mr. Joseph Scott, of Los Angeles, California, is now ready to be sent to you. However, we are wondering whether you are in need of this affidavit and documentation. Will you kindly inform us in this matter as soon as possible?"

There that line of communications ends. We do know that Papa had told Miss Rieff that an affidavit was not enough for entry since the quota for Hungarians was full. Papa had said that what was needed, beyond an affidavit, was a specific job offer. Father Ostermann had written earlier that the committee had great success placing doctors once they were in the United States. They seemed to be ships passing in the night. In any event the letter trail with the committee ends there.

Papa Saves a Life

One day, when Mutti returned from giving a lesson, Papa greeted her with a big smile on his face. "I am very happy," he announced. "I saved a life today."

"What happened?" Mutti asked.

Papa explained that the landlady had rushed in and said someone needed a doctor right away at the big hotel down the avenue. He grabbed his bag, rushed there and found a woman having a serious asthma attack. Fortunately, he happened to have the appropriate medicine and gave her an injection. It was just what she needed and not a moment to spare. She soon came round and her husband was very grateful. Papa said they were an English couple by the name of Becker.

"That's a funny name for an Englishman. Did you get paid?" Mutti asked.

"No, but it was wonderful to do what I was trained to do and get such a satisfying result," he said.

Mutti asked, "Doesn't it seem odd to you that someone in a fancy hotel would go to a boarding house to look for a doctor? Something about this seems wrong."

Papa laughed it off. But this incident was to have repercussions.

Starting School

It must have been the committee that arranged for me to enter a new school in Rio. I heard Papa tell Mutti that it was an expensive school but that the priests were accepting me without payment.

The school was a Catholic grammar school for boys, named after a saintly young boy, Guy de Fontgalland, who had died young. His portrait hung in the entry hall, showing him in a white communion suit with an armband from which white ribbons fluttered. The school was in a residential area, on a wide street divided by an island with flowers. Thick grass lined the sidewalks.

I did my best to fit in. Even though we had been in Brazil for only three months, my Portuguese was good; Lisl and I learned it quickly and had local accents. My parents, on the other hand, though each spoke several languages, had to work to learn Portuguese, and continued to speak with a distinct German accent. But I was way behind in local culture. The boys would speak about sports stars, or movie stars, or some current event, and I really had no idea what or who they were talking about.

My European clothes were also different, heavier than those of the other boys, and all I had were short pants. The other boys wore long pants. And many of the boys were picked up by cars, often driven by chauffeurs. Mutti came to take me home on the trolley. Still, many boys were friendly.

The school featured a big open backyard where we could run

and kick soccer balls. On one side, a big tree provided welcome shade. On the other side, the back of a church bordered the yard. We periodically went into the church to mark some special day or other.

Two people made a big difference for me at the school. The first was my teacher, a young woman named Dona Teresinha, with dark hair and sparkling eyes. I liked her very much and enjoyed being in her classroom. But I had heard that a young man often met her after school and that he was her fiancé. One afternoon after school, she walked with me to the garden in the front. She took my hand, crouched down beside me and asked, "Why don't you smile at me? Why do you seem glum?" I muttered something about my clothes and short pants, but I think what she perceived was more likely my discomfort at trying to fit in as an outsider.

"Oh, don't worry about that," she said. "There are so many Europeans coming that soon all the boys will wear short pants. Besides, the other boys wear long pants so they don't have to wash their legs." I wasn't sure whether to believe that, but it was an intriguing new idea.

"Don't you like me?" she asked. I stammered something about the young man waiting for her. "Oh, don't worry about him. He's very sweet, but you and I can still be good friends." I blushed as I said, "Thank you," and waved goodbye to her.

Just then, Father Alfonso came by, almost as if he'd been watching us. The other important person in my school life, he often talked to me and I liked being with him. "How's my little storyteller?" he asked. "That was a very good story you told me," he said, referring to a story I had told him that I had heard from Mutti.

"You should hear my mother," I replied. "She is really good."

"Well," he said, "I think you could write some stories and maybe you could sell them and earn enough to buy some ice cream."

"That would be nice, but I'd really like to earn more," I replied.

"And what would you do with more?" he asked.

"I'd buy a house," I said.

"Wow. That would take a lot of stories. Why do you want to buy a house? Did you own a house in Vienna?" he asked.

"No, we didn't," I answered, "We lived in an apartment but my grandmother owns her house. If you own a house, you own the ground under it and if you own the ground, then you own a piece of the country and then they can't throw you out."

"That's very interesting," Father Alfonso replied. "I don't think I've ever heard it expressed that way before. Were you thrown out of Austria?"

"Yes, we were," I answered. "Papa had to leave because he was Hungarian and Mutti and my sister and I came with him."

"Could you explain that to me?" Father Alfonso asked.

I was a little surprised. Father Alfonso was a smart man. I was surprised that he did not understand what I'd said. But I really admired him and I wanted to be his friend. So I explained it to him again.

"Well," I said, "when the Germans came to Vienna, all my uncles and aunts — everybody — was talking about being Aryan. And I realized that Aryan meant German. They only wanted Germans there now. I heard someone say they were sending people to prison if they weren't Aryan Germans. I knew my father and his whole family were Hungarians and the next thing I knew Papa had left very quickly. I put it together and realized that he had to leave because he was Hungarian and not Aryan."

"But your family are all Catholics, aren't they?" Father Alfonso asked again.

"Of course," I said. "Everybody I know is Catholic." Now I was really surprised that he had trouble understanding what I had said. "It's not whether you are Catholic, but whether you are Aryan, whether you are a German like the Germans. The Austrians all speak German and so I think that made the Austrians Aryan too, but my father was Hungarian." I raised my voice a little on the word "Hungarian" just to emphasize it.

"Thank you for that explanation," Father Alfonso said. "I think I understand it now. Thank you."

"I'm glad," I said. "Mutti will be happy that I was able to explain it all."

"That was a lot of good work," Father Alfonso said. "Let's get back to the idea that you might write a book of stories. Tell you what, why don't we walk to the plaza and get an ice cream and we can talk about how you can do a book." He took me by the hand, and we walked three blocks to a big square, which had an ice cream shop.

The square had a park in the middle and a movie house on one side. I remember once even going to a movie — *The Mark of Zorro*. It made a deep impression on me. The hero was so heroic and good-looking, and his sword flashed as he made his mark of "Z." I was inspired and could only hope that someday I would be as dashing and brave and make my mark on the world.

The Brazilians love soccer. Kids everywhere kick balls — and anything else that will roll — all the time. Each district in Rio had its own team and there was a fierce rivalry something like the Dodgers, Giants and Yankees used to have in New York City. We lived in Ipanema and the colors of our team were red and black. One of my treasured possessions was a small net you wore on your head with the Ipanema team colors.

Soccer had also been a favorite sport in Austria and Hungary. My father befriended a Hungarian who was the coach of the Botafogo team. I was introduced to him once. We did not see any professional soccer games in Rio, but while we lived in Vienna my father took me to a stadium to see a game. I remember the huge crowd of people in the stands. My father was an enthusiastic fan, and when our team scored he got so excited that he threw his hat in the air. I doubt he ever got it back. He probably didn't mind.

A Disappointment; a New Possibility

It was late March when Papa was notified that a letter from England had arrived for him at the committee's office. "Sweetheart," he said to Mutti, "this could be what we have been waiting for, the visa to England. Give me a kiss and say a prayer." He came back a few hours later, walking slowly, dejected.

Mutti, seeing him, ran to him and asked, "What's the matter?"

"It's all over. They've cancelled the visa to England."

Papa handed Mutti two letters, one from Mr. Ellis and the other from the British Home Office. The letter from Mr. Ellis read, "Mrs. Kapp of The Coordinating Committee for Refugees has written us as follows: 'Further to our letter to you of the 7th March, we informed the Home Office of Dr. Weiser's change of address, and they have replied as per the enclosed copy letter which we send for your perusal.'"

Mutti quickly turned to the Home Office letter. The heading was "Home Office (Aliens Dept)." It read, "Dear Mrs. Kapp, With reference to your letter of the 3rd instant, about the case of Dr. Arthur Weiser who is now in Brazil with his family, we think it would be best for him to stay there and to give up the idea of taking a British qualification with a view to eventual practice in Kenya. Although Mr. R. Loy undertakes to help him, when qualified, to establish himself in Kenya, it is by no means certain that he will be able to implement this undertaking, indeed it is highly improbable.

In view of these considerations and of the stringent policy here in regard to the admission of foreign doctors, if only to qualify, we feel that Dr. Weiser should give up the idea and try to settle down in Brazil where there is presumably scope for him to do so."

"Mother in Heaven!" Mutti cried out. She leaned against Papa to steady herself. "I don't believe it." She was near tears.

Papa put his arms around Mutti. "We just have to face that what we had is gone," he said. "All that work and the tremendous efforts by Bruce, Ellis, Loy, and Mrs. Kapp. It's all gone and we are left in Brazil."

Looking back now, it is not hard to comprehend how devastating a blow the Home Office denial must have been. The guarantee from Mr. Loy had been received and accepted by the British authorities. The visa to enter England had been issued. All that remained was a simple administrative step of forwarding the document to Brazil. And then it was snatched away.

The last realistic hope to settle somewhere and practice medicine was suddenly gone, taken by a bureaucrat who perhaps honestly, but mistakenly, thought Papa "should settle down in Brazil where there is presumably scope for him" to practice medicine. Of course, that bureaucrat was a busy man with hundreds of equally pressing and deserving applications before him. But he made an uninformed decision about our circumstances in Brazil and unfortunately for us it was wrong. It very much changed the direction of our lives. It must have taken Papa and Mutti quite a while to recover but they always put on a brave and optimistic face for Lisl and me. We were never aware of the blows they suffered.

But when things appear darkest, a ray of light sometimes shines through. So it was that Papa received a call from a Dr. Campos, who had gotten Papa's name from the committee. He had an active medical practice and wanted to see whether there was some way he might help my father. He invited Papa to come to his office to discuss possibilities. Dr. Campos's license would cover Papa as they worked together. It seemed like a genuine breakthrough.

When Papa returned from his meeting with Dr. Campos, Mutti was waiting at the door. "Well," she asked, "how did it go?"

"Dr. Campos is a friendly and decent person," Papa said. "And he wants to help. I'm just not sure how it will work."

"What do you mean?" Mutti asked.

"It took me a while to understand what he had in mind. He certainly has patients, but the office is really geared for only one doctor. There is only one consulting office and only one examining room. Two of us working at the same time would be quite difficult. And there is the issue of patients. Campos is a family doctor and some of his patients have been with him for years. He would not want to shift any of those patients to me, especially since my Portuguese is questionable. It's fine for everyday life but I am still learning the technical medical language. Eventually I realized he was offering me the opportunity to develop my own practice treating patients from the refugee community; they would prefer someone who spoke their language. Campos is giving me a real opportunity to treat my patients under the cover of his status as a Brazilian doctor. The burden will now be on me to find enough patients to support us. That will not be easy. Even if I find patients, most of them, like us, can barely pay their rent."

The Burjans and the Baron

I t was, I think, Father Alfonso who arranged the invitation for my parents to visit the Burjans. They were a wealthy Viennese couple who lived on the top floor in a corner apartment overlooking the ocean in Rio. Mr. Burjan had been a senior officer in the Austrian telephone company, but his wife persuaded him to leave Austria well before Hitler arrived. It was also his wife who persuaded him to buy property in Switzerland that provided them a steady income. They also owned a *fazenda* ("plantation" in Portuguese) that grew coffee. They lived in another world.

My parents had visited them once before. This time, Lisl and I were also invited for a Sunday lunch.

When we arrived, Mr. Burjan welcomed us. He was a short, stocky man with a light, well-cut suit that hung generously over his thick waist. He was bald and wore pince-nez glasses. He kissed my mother's hand, shook my father's hand, and showed us into the living room, which was bright with light from big windows and French doors that opened onto a small balcony.

Mrs. Burjan rose, smiling, as we entered the room. Her dark braided hair circled the top of her head like the edge of a dark halo. Her dress was subdued, simple, and well-fitted. I later heard that she had been a nun, or perhaps a nurse, who had tended to Mr. Burjan's first wife during a long illness that eventually ended in her death. In time, she and Mr. Burjan married. Many years later, I

Papa and Mutti visiting the apartment of the Burjans in Rio.

heard that she was a pious woman, and indeed so pious that some people said she should be made a saint.

She suggested that perhaps Lisl and I would like to look out from the balcony. I certainly did. I vividly remember standing with my mother and my sister on the balcony looking out toward the sea. The view was beautiful — we saw the blue ocean turning green as it approached the shore and cresting in waves that crashed in a blanket of white foam. You could watch it for hours.

Mrs. Burjan asked Papa, "Does your visa expire in a month?"

Papa was surprised she knew that. But Mrs. Burjan said they knew the Austrian expatriate community in Rio well. "My husband and I do not have much else to do."

I was excited about lunch because it was going to be *feijoada*, which I loved and got only rarely. Feijoada is the classic Brazilian black bean casserole with chunks of meats and sausage. You eat it with rice or tapioca. Here we had rice and it was delicious. The meal ended with ice cream. It was a feast.

Two weeks later, the Burjans invited my parents to dinner again. This was an evening event for adults only. They intended to have my parents meet a baron and baroness. Baron Ludwig Kummer, Mutti told Lisl and me when she got home, was an Austrian from an old family in Salzburg. He was planning to build a factory north of Rio to make tapioca flour. The baron intended to take advantage of a new Brazilian decree designed to encourage the use of tapioca: The new law required that all flour used for baking had to include at least 30 percent tapioca flour. That created a whole new market for tapioca, a product native to Brazil. The baron was putting together the pieces to get his project going.

As Mutti described it, the baron swept into the apartment in a burst of energy. He headed for Mr. Burjan and gave him a hug and then moved toward Mrs. Burjan. Then he saw my parents and asked the Burjans to introduce him. He was a tall man who kept moving around the room and could not sit still. Asked about his project, he said, "I have all the money I need. What I need now are some good people; someone who knows the government and others who can help run the operation."

Mrs. Burjan noted that there was another guest coming that evening, a man named Kolszinski. As Kolszinski had been an ambassador and had good contacts, the baron felt he might fill the slot for government relations.

Papa began asking questions about the project and the baron looked at him with more interest. He asked if Papa knew chemistry. "Yes, as a matter of fact, I do," Papa answered. "My uncle is a professor of chemistry at the University of Budapest. I like chemistry and sat in on many of his classes."

Then Papa asked about the health of the local population. The baron answered that malaria was the main problem.

Papa said, "I've read that the Rockefeller Institute for Medical Research in New York has done a lot of research on tropical diseases. If you have no objection, I could write the Rockefeller Institute and see if they have any information on health in Brazil and see if they have any solutions to suggest."

"Good man," cried the baron, "great idea. Let me know what you find out."

With that, the baron thanked his hostess and left. Mrs. Burjan turned to Papa and said, "He's quite interested in you. Better keep your eyes open. He is quite a salesman."

On the way home, Papa said, "That baron is really dynamic, he's a bundle of energy and his wife is a charming woman." Mutti, normally optimistic, was more cautious. "Actually I found the baron's wife a bit cold and not very friendly, and the baron certainly has big ideas but I wonder how well thought out they are."

A few days later, Papa received an invitation from the baron to come by his hotel. When Papa returned and told Mutti about the meeting, she said, "I think Mrs. Burjan was right. He's got his eye on you and will keep probing to see if you are someone for his project."

A week later there was a message asking Papa to go see the baron. When he returned, he told Mutti that he was getting more interested in tapioca and the baron's project.

Baron Ludwig Kummer in an undated photo.

"Did he ask you more about your experience?" Mutti asked.

"Yes, as a matter of fact, he did," Papa replied. "We discussed my time in the army and talked about the papers I wrote for medical journals and the doctors who were my mentors as I progressed in my career. And he also wanted my views on some matters involving chemistry and on other matters involving personnel and health conditions."

"Sounds like he's trying to assess your abilities," Mutti observed. She added, "You are a very intelligent person and you have a good way with people. You did a lot of work on your grandfather's farm and I am sure you learned a lot that would apply here. The reason the baron keeps talking with you is because he sees the possibilities."

Papa ended their chat, saying, "It is fun to talk to the man and to learn about his plans. But if we weren't so desperately short of money, I'd never consider working in the backcountry as a manager of an industrial plant. I'd much, much rather continue to look for an opportunity to practice medicine, like with that young doctor from southern Brazil. But it's been months now and who knows if and when another opportunity like that might come along?"

That evening Mutti put Lisl and me to bed and told us one of her good stories. Lisl went to sleep right away but I lay there. I couldn't quite fall asleep. After a few minutes, Mutti said, "Papa has gone again to speak with the baron at his hotel. I want you to lie there quietly and keep an eye on Lisl, while I go out briefly to see how Papa is doing. Then I'll be right back."

I said okay and lay there quietly, watching the changing patterns on the ceiling. I listened to Lisl's quiet breathing and to the sounds from the street. I couldn't fall asleep. Time went by and still I lay awake. It seemed like a long time and I began to worry about Mutti. She should have been home by now. Maybe something happened on her way home. The more I thought about it, the more worried I became.

I decided to go look for her. I got up, got dressed, checked on Lisl and closed the door gently. Then I walked out into the street. Papa had taken me by the baron's hotel a few days earlier and I had a good sense of direction. The hotel was not that far away. I thought I'd meet Mutti on her way home.

But first I had to cross the avenue in front of the house. Papa and Mutti had said that I should only cross with an adult. I looked around. There were people on the street but most were walking up or down the avenue and not across it. Finally I saw a man on the corner. He seemed a little unsteady but I went up to him. "Can I help you across the street?" I asked.

"Well, sonny," he slurred, "isn't that nice. Yes, you can help me."

He gave me his arm. I looked both ways and when the street was clear I guided him across. He shuffled to a nearby lamppost, leaned on it and waved goodbye to me.

I kept walking. I knew that first I followed the trolley tracks down toward the ocean. Walking along the avenue was fine; it was well lighted and there were people around. But then I had to turn right into a residential street. It got quieter and darker. I knew that I had to go at least two more long blocks and then turn right again and follow the street up the hill to the hotel. Those blocks were deserted and seemed very long and very dark. I walked as fast as I could. Finally, I came to the corner and up ahead, up the hill, I could see the lighted front door of the hotel.

My legs pumped away and soon I was there. I went in the front door and met a man in the entry. "Could you please tell me which is the baron's apartment?"

"You are out kind of late, young man," he said, "but yes. I can tell you. It's apartment C. I'll walk you there."

At the apartment, the doorman rang the bell. The baron answered, saw the two of us and said, "Harry, what have you brought me?" And then he looked down at me and laughed. "What are you doing here? Shouldn't you be in bed?"

When he led me in, my parents were shocked and Mutti immediately became worried. "Hansi, what's matter? Why are you here? Is Lisl all right?" She gave me a hard embrace. The party broke up as my parents immediately took me home. There was not much talk as we hurried home. Mutti was really worried about Lisl.

When we got to the avenue, we could see the landlord across the street in front of the house. He was shouting my name, "Hansi, Hansi!" Papa called out to him and when he saw the three of us, he said, "Thank goodness. You found him."

My mom said, "Where is Lisl?" He answered that she was still in bed. My mother almost trotted to the house and then we heard a scream, "She's not here." We all ran into the house and began looking. Mutti went up to the main floor — and there was Lisl. She was sound asleep, nestled in the arms of the big black woman who worked at the house. Mutti said that Lisl's blond hair against the jet black of the woman's arm and the blue of her dress made a beautiful picture. As the woman handed Lisl to Mutti, she said, "That's one of the nicest hours I've had in a long time." So we all went to bed.

The next morning, Lisl told us that she had awakened, seen that I was missing and started looking for me around the house. That alerted the landlord to start searching for me outside.

Fun Times in Rio

A few days later, Papa came home and said, "Get dressed, kids, you are going to a party."

"Where are we going?" I asked.

He said, "It's a party for children of Hungarian refugees in Rio."

"But you are not a Hungarian citizen," I said.

"Here it's enough that I was born in Hungary," he laughed. "Don't argue. Just get ready."

Mutti got us cleaned up; we got on the trolley and headed to the party.

Hansi in sailor's suit and Lisl, opposite him, at a party for children of Hungarian refugees in Rio in March 1939.

We arrived at a white stucco house overlooking a park and were led upstairs to a large terrace festooned with paper streamers. Colorful napkins and plates were arranged around a table and there was a big tub filled with water for bobbing for apples. There were four other children. I was the oldest. The hostess and Mutti coordinated the apple-bobbing. We played "pin the tail on the donkey" and then we were ready for ice cream. It was a wonderful change from the routine and the food at the boarding house and a nice day out with other children.

Mutti told me that there were also social events for adult refugees at a community room in downtown Rio. She went several times, and it was there she learned that Count Morazevsky was himself a refugee.

Rio has a magnificent physical setting. Two spectacular beaches, Copacabana and Ipanema, are separated by the iconic Sugar Loaf Mountain. The beaches are the first things you see as you approach by ship. At the far end of Ipanema, there is another mountain, the anvil-shaped Gavea Mountain.

Other mountains rise behind the city, the most dramatic being Corcovado ("hunchback" in Portuguese), named for the shape of the base of the mountain. Its granite peak rises straight up, almost 2,400 feet high. At the top stands the internationally famous huge white statue of Christ with his hands outstretched. The statue is over 100 feet tall and is illuminated at night. In the dark of night, the illuminated Christ appears to be floating in the sky.

There is a narrow road to the top of Corcovado. One Sunday, friends who had a car gave us a ride up. It was thrilling to stand at the foot of the statue. The views stretched out across the city and over several bays leading toward the ocean; it was breathtaking.

On another memorable trip, we drove north from Rio around the bay to a beach on the ocean. The group included another boy, a few years older than me. We arrived at a deserted beach with a few large boulders by the shore. We swam in the ocean and then clambered on the rocks, which were too high for us to dive from. As we watched the water, we suddenly noticed that one of the underwater "rocks" was moving away. It looked big to me. We ran back and told everybody what we had seen. We learned that the "rock" was probably a sting ray. Just as well that we hadn't jumped in.

The mountains behind Rio rise fairly high and as the altitude increases, the temperature moderates. The mountains also catch some breeze and have large wooded, shady areas. People who can afford it have cabins in those mountains to escape the heat of the city. I remember standing with Lisl and a group of adults next to the porch of a house surrounded by a thick stand of trees with a saddled horse nearby. It was nice to have friends of friends invite you to their house in the country.

A Third Boarding House

A t the boarding house on Avenida Isabel, where we were living, the landlord's wife left her husband and the boarding house. After she left, things began to go downhill more and more. Papa decided we should move and began to look for another place. He thought he might at least inquire at a boarding house overlooking the beach in Ipanema. My parents had often walked by the grand house of this two-building complex and remarked that it must be the place where wealthier refugees lived. It turned out to cost only a small amount more than the house we were in. We moved quickly and happily. Mutti later remarked that we had been living in a cave for a year. I think it was closer to six months but I guess she really found it depressing.

The main building, where a number of tenants lived, held the kitchen and common dining room. We lived in the separate two-story cottage about a block and a half away. The neighborhood was a quiet residential suburb. Small houses lined the street, shaded by trees and often surrounded by gardens. It was only a few blocks from the trolley that took me to school.

Our room was on the ground floor of the cottage, which was surrounded by grass and shrubs. Three other families, all Jewish refugees, shared the cottage with us. When we arrived, one of the women there came to see Mutti and told her she would wash on Thursdays. The women in the cottage had worked out arrangements to allocate jobs and share responsibility. There were limitations on using water but they had devised systems where water was used more than once.

When Mutti went out to teach, some of the resident women watched us. Others might take us to school if neither of our parents was available. In exchange, my parents would help them by doing some errand or other for them. In fact, as one of these mutual favors, Mutti began bleaching the hair of one of the other women, even though she had never done it before. Mutti thought she might be able to persuade the woman to stop bleaching her hair by convincing her that she would look better with darker hair. She suc-

Mutti, Hansi and Lisl at the entrance of the boarding house in Ipanema, Rio, January 1940.

ceeded only too well. The woman decided she wanted to have black hair. Mutti found out that dyeing hair black is a lot messier.

From my point of view, the move to our new home was wonderful because it was just half a block from the beach. The Danube and the sheltered arm of water where we swam at Kuchelau did not have waves or a mile of sand. I had never played on a beach before. Furthermore, I could go whenever I could get Mutti or another adult at the house to watch me at the beach. I learned how to jump in the waves and eventually learned to bodysurf. I'm sure my most successful ride lasted only a few seconds, but it was a thrill to be held up by the wave and to be carried forward with foam bubbling at my throat. I had to time my jump just right to catch the wave so it would carry me along. There were many misses but the worst that happened was that I just jumped around in the warm water a little more. Then I'd enjoy a successful ride. Exhilarating! We learned that a red flag posted by the lifeguards meant a dangerous undertow and to stay out of the water.

In addition to the water and the waves, the sandy beach extended all around. You could run in the sand, fall in it or just watch it make patterns as the waves washed up and receded. We built sand castles. It was a wonderful playground.

We spent a lot of time walking barefoot. Paralleling the beach was a walkway with a beautiful large black and white pattern. You quickly learned that black tiles got very hot and that you had to walk on the white tiles.

It was on the beach that I also remember meeting a girl of about 7, like me. Her name was Linda and that might be as close to a first girlfriend as I had. I'm not sure what she thought, but I looked for her when I got to the beach and enjoyed playing near her or with her.

A Painful Lesson

One day Papa gave me a penny and asked me to go to the store across the street and buy him a book of matches. The store owner was down at the far end of the store's long counter chatting with a customer. I stood by the counter near the door where the matches were. I waited and waited and waited. The owner just kept chatting and did not pay any attention to me. The matches were right in front of me. Finally, I took a book of matches and brought it to Papa.

I kept the penny in my shirt pocket. It must have clinked against something else in my pocket.

The cat was out of the bag.

When Papa heard about it, he asked Mutti to take Lisl to dinner at the other building. Then he laid me across his lap and smacked me on the bottom with his belt. "Never, ever steal again," he scolded.

I was 7 at the time and Papa spanking me made a lifelong impression. Papa had never spanked me before. I only remember him hitting me once and that was a quick cuff on the head when I had made a disparaging comment to my grandmother. He taught by how he behaved.

The Baron Makes an Offer

P apa had gone to talk with Baron Kummer again. When he returned, he looked serious. Mutti gave him a hello kiss and asked, "How did it go?"

"Well, he's offered me a job managing the factory and promised to build a house for us in Barra," Papa replied.

"That's wonderful," Mutti said.

Papa was unsure. He felt he lacked the correct experience but Mutti reassured him: "The baron thinks you can do it. He respects your ability. He's a shrewd judge of people. He sees an intelligent, disciplined person who works hard."

"I'll probably take the offer," Papa answered. "But I've told the baron I need few days to think about it."

A few days later, Papa came home with a smile on his face. "Guess who I saw today?" he asked my mother.

"I don't know. Who?" she asked.

"Mr. Becker. Remember the lady with asthmatic seizure whose life I think I saved? Becker is her husband," Papa explained.

"Yes, I remember," Mutti said. "The Englishman with the German name."

"Well, he couldn't have been nicer." Papa said. "He offered to have me join him tonight at the casino for some roulette and champagne."

"But he didn't offer to pay for your services," Mutti snapped.

Papa continued. "No, but then he asked me if I could recommend some young men to join him as salesmen in the South of Brazil. They'd be door-to-door salesmen and he mentioned a big pay package — several thousand *cruzeiros* a month and a commission on sales."

Mutti jumped in, "Wow! That's so rich it sounds fishy."

"Well, it sounded so good that I asked him if I could have the job myself. After all, it seems like less of a long-term commitment than working for the baron in Barra. But Becker turned me down, saying I wasn't really suited for it. So I gave him the names of two young immigrant men I met through the count. And so we parted."

"However," Papa continued, "something about moving to Barra has been bothering me. Living in Barra is going to be very different from living in Rio. This is a big city with all the advantages of a big city — lots of people, the Burjans, people at the Hungarian club, other Europeans, we have the beach nearby. It's true that we'd be better off financially in Barra but we'd also be more alone; there are few people there who share our background and education. And two of them are the baron and the baroness and they are a group unto themselves. In a sense, we'd be very isolated."

Mutti answered quickly. "Look, I just want to be with you and the children. That's all I need. I can do without other people if I have to. And I would definitely not enjoy Rio if you weren't here."

Papa left but Mutti continued to stand there and look out the window quietly. I knew she was thinking about a lot of things.

A few hours later, Papa returned. He was not as excited as I thought he might be. The baron wanted him to go to Barra right away. "He wants me in Barra to oversee the construction. You'll come with the children as soon as we can organize housing for all of us."

"Where are you going to live?" Mutti asked.

"Kolszinski and I will live in the baron's house," Papa said.

"Kolszinski will be a partner in ownership of the plant with the baron."

Mutti was quiet. She finally said, "I'm glad you are taking the job and I'll do the best I can. Being separated is going to be very hard. I don't want to be separated from you. What I want is your love and the children's love. Beside that I just need a little food, almost no companionship and ten hours of sleep."

Papa said quietly, "The thought of being without you for a long time made me very sad. There is no greater gift than to have someone love you. I am so glad we have each other."

Papa Goes to Work for the Baron

So Papa started going out every morning, all dressed up and returning late in the day. I heard him say to Mutti that he was buying equipment for the plant's laboratory, as well as other special measuring equipment. The baron had sent him money and a list of items. Now Papa was busy going to stores that sold equipment, finding which had the best wares and negotiating good prices. Mutti said he did better shopping for the baron than he had ever done for himself.

The weeks flew by and in mid-October Papa left for Barra de Itapaboana, the village where the baron was building the tapioca mill. I heard that it was a long train ride and then a long ride in a truck to get there. I missed him right away.

A week after Papa had left, Mutti received the first letter from him.

Mutti unfolded the letter and sat down; Lisl and I stood, one on either side, looking at the paper with writing that neither of us could yet read.

"My dearest Bunny," Mutti began reading, then looked up and added, "and my dear children." She returned to the letter.

It is a beautiful Sunday in Barra and I have a
few free minutes to write you. I arrived safely and
am living in the baron's house. It has many rooms,

all opening onto a long corridor down the middle. Two of the rooms are ours, until they build us a new house. You'll like where the house is going to be built. It's down the road from the baron's house, on a small rise with a thick-trunked tree with glossy leaves and large, crimson flowers. Little hummingbirds fly from blossom to blossom, their iridescence shining in the sunlight. Beyond the tree, fields stretch to the horizon and to mountains in the distance. It's a lovely spot.

"We're going to have our own, new house. Did you hear that?" I interrupted.

"Let me keep reading," Mutti said.

From the room where I am writing, I can see the river that flows by the house to the ocean; it is sparkling with sunlight. In the sparkles you sometimes see floating islands of water lilies, white and purple, coasting downriver. A very high tide must have raised the lily pads until the roots could no longer hold, and freed them to float on.

Across the river, the far bank is a long spit of sand dunes that separates the river from the sea. When the wind blows from the ocean you hear the waves crashing on the beach. The beach, I've heard, is as sandy as Ipanema, but unlike Ipanema it stretches as far as the eye can see. On holidays the people at the house often row a boat across the river to go swimming in the ocean.

You will also enjoy seeing the flights of birds that rise like a small cloud of white from the trees across the river. A long thin island runs parallel to the far bank. The island is heavily treed and large white birds roost on the tops of the trees. Every now and then you hear the flapping of wings as they fly off together, circle a few times and gently settle down again.

Dearest Bunny, I hope you and the children can join me soon. Give the rascals a big hug for me. I am sending you a thousand kisses, your loving, lonely husband, Arthur."

After Mutti read the letter, she asked Lisl and me, "Children, did you have any idea that Papa was a poet?"

"What's a poet?" I asked.

"Someone who can describe nature and people in ways that make us feel the beauty and wonder of things," Mutti replied. "Papa is a wonderful doctor. But the letter we just read is as beautiful as any poet could write."

"Barra sounds like a beautiful place," I said.

"Yes, it does," said my mother quietly.

A few days later another letter arrived. Mutti sat down and let us listen as she read.

Dearest Bunny, all is going well. You will enjoy the pageantry of dinner here. It is a formal event. The table is set with the baroness's fine china and crystal glasses on a fine table cloth. It is as though they are recreating life in Salzburg. You might almost believe it, until you look out the window and realize you are in small tropical village.

Dinner is served by Kolszinski's Negro butler wearing white gloves. Usually only five of us are at dinner because the baron travels almost all the time. So we have the baroness, her 15-year-old daughter, a sweet child, Kolszinski, Franzen, the plant's accountant, and me. You may remember Kolszinski from the Burjans'. He is the baron's partner and was formerly in the diplomatic corps. He generally wears crisp jodhpurs and spit-shined shoes. It helps that he has a butler.

Outside things are moving quickly. Construction of the mill is in full swing. They have already poured the concrete for the foundation. Bulldozers are pushing earth and lifting it onto trucks to take away. On the river, a barge arrives regularly, bringing bricks for the chimney. And there are men moving everywhere. There is a sense of purpose in the air, a big change for what had been a sleepy waterfront village.

I send you many hugs and kisses and long to see your face. I hope you can come soon. Love, your Arthur.

Then, a few days later, another letter came, but this one was from the baroness. Mutti read it to herself. As she read it, her face darkened. I moved closer to her. When she finished, she lowered the letter and looked out the window. She looked concerned.

"What is it, Mutti?" I asked.

"Nothing, sweetheart," she replied.

"You look unhappy," I said.

"You are an alert little boy," she laughed as she tousled my hair.

"Well?" I looked up at her.

"It's nice that the baroness would write," she said, "but she makes Barra seem very difficult."

"But Papa wrote us how beautiful it was," I said.

"That's right."

"What did she say that makes you unhappy?" I asked.

"Your father is a very honest person, so you can believe what he says," Mutti said. "I read you his letter and he made Barra sound like a very pleasant place. The baroness wrote that it was good that I wasn't there because Barra was very hot, it was humid, there were many mosquitoes and she actually saw a snake. She wrote that it was good that I was in Rio. It looks like the baron is in no rush for us to move. He probably won't move us if the baroness thinks it's better that we stay here."

Letters from Papa were arriving every few days.

Dearest Sweetheart, It is a quiet Sunday and I took advantage of the day off to take a long walk. I started in the early morning cool, just as dawn was breaking. I followed the road, really a wide path that leads away from the river and heads to the mountains in the distance. It was good to walk at a steady pace, to feel muscles warming, the heart beating and, yes, some perspiration. You feel alive with the steady movement and your mind calms in the quiet rhythm. I thought of the many happy walks we have had together — those pleasant walks in the woods around Vienna and the challenging but satisfying hikes in the Dolomites where we had our honeymoon. We have had some wonderful times together. Come soon, your husband misses you and wants to share some of the delights here. Give the children many kisses from me and I send you a thousand more, Your perspiring husband, Arthur.

Another week passed and another letter from Papa arrived.

> Dearest Bunny, I am tired, but happy. There is so much to learn, and many men to supervise. Construction begins when the sun rises to get as much done as possible before the heat becomes too much. There is a long mid-day break and the men rest in whatever shade they can find; then they start again in mid-afternoon on and continue working until dinnertime. I ask a lot of questions. I want to learn as much as I can about the mill — how it will work, what the different parts do. It's something that engineers know but it wasn't what I learned at medical school or in my practice. I'm also getting to know the men who will stay on as mill hands when the plant is finished and operations begin.
>
> I am also getting to know the pharmacist. He was the key man in town before the baron came, but he is still the most important man in town for the villagers. I call him the pharmacist but he plays many other roles. He handles a lot of basic medical matters; he is the notary and handles contracts and, before the baron came, he had the only car in town. His shop has a wide set of steps outside, with people standing on them all day long. Some are there to gossip but most are there for one or more of his services. Of course if the baron or his family or the European workers here don't feel well, they will see me. The pharmacist would not expect to treat them. But I also want to be sure that if I am called by a villager, the pharmacist won't object.
>
> It's good to be working, although most of it is

not medicine. I am happy that I can send money for you and the children. I really did not like scrambling all the time to scratch enough cash together to pay the landlord.

Dear Sweetheart, I miss you terribly and miss the little rascals. Hugs for everybody and a special sweet kiss for you, your Arthur.

The next letter came only a few days later.

My sweet Honeybunny, I hope you will find Barra as interesting as I do. There is a lot to learn but it is also exciting to see the changes that the project is making here. When I walk from the baron's house into the village, I enter another world. It is a world that has changed very little in a hundred years. The roads are unpaved; transportation is by oxcart or by horse-drawn wagons. There are a few solid houses of brick and stucco near the waterfront but as you move back from the river the houses are made of mud with thatched roofs. The people are friendly and gracious but have little formal education. Now the baron has brought in trucks and other mechanized equipment for the plant. The plant will provide jobs for workers there and create demand from the local farms to grow steady crops of cassava root [the source of tapioca] to supply the plant. I heard Kolszinski say that the whole enterprise might support as many as 3,000 people. That would have a big effect on the region around our village, a village that has at most a few hundred people.

A few days later and another letter came. Lisl and I stood by Mutti as she opened and read it. It was just a page long.

> Dearest Bunny, Work on the mill continues steadily. You can see change from day to day. The foundations have been poured and they have begun work on the footings for the walls. The chimney is slowly rising. From my room, I can see the men working on a shipyard down the river. It has a large shed open at one end and a dock with several cranes. The baron plans to build a ship there. Knowing the baron, if he has one, he'll want two. Two days ago a heavy rain turned the roads to mud. Every few hours, we had to collect a crew to free a truck stuck in the mud. But today the sun is strong and things are drying out. Here at the house, the news is that the administrative manager's wife is coming. She will stay with the daughter while the baroness is away traveling with the baron. The baroness will be away almost two weeks.
>
> Dearest Bunny, I miss you and the children every day. Give them both big hugs for me. I send you a thousand kisses and look forward to having you here soon, your loving, longing-for-you, husband, Arthur.

When she finished, Mutti put the letter down slowly and was quiet. That was unusual. Mutti was a happy person. Papa's letters usually cheered her up and made her even happier. This time she was just very quiet, turned to the window but wasn't really looking.

"What's the matter?" I asked.

She looked at me, paused and then said, "You noticed. You are right. Something in the letter worries me."

"What is it?" I asked.

"The part about the administrative manager's wife going to Barra to baby-sit the daughter while the baroness is away," she said. "What concerns me is the idea that the administrative manager's wife comes for a time to Barra and then returns to Rio, as if Rio is where she is supposed to live. You would think that a wife should be with her husband. I worry that if they think it's a good thing for the administrative manager's wife to live in Rio, they might also think it's a good thing for me to live in Rio. And I really want to be with Papa and to have us all together."

The idea that I might not see Papa for a long time upset me too. I thought about it and then something occurred to me. "But Papa said that they were going to build a house for us. That must mean that we'll all be in Barra," I said.

"Well, you're right. Let's pray that they meant what they said about the house and that we won't have to wait too long for it to be built," Mutti answered.

Becker, Again

While we were waiting for more news from Barra, a problem arose in Rio.

Mutti had left early one morning to teach another English lesson. She was in a good mood. She had been teaching long enough to become comfortable and to enjoy it and she was happy to be earning money. She also enjoyed the brisk walk to the trolley. It was only four blocks but she could really step out when she didn't have to walk at the same pace as Lisl and I did. Mainly, she just liked being out in the open. She had gotten used to the bold colors and larger-than-life flowers of the tropics. And she enjoyed mingling with the people on the street and the movement of the trolley.

When Mutti returned, the landlord, Roberto, was waiting for her with alarming news. "You were lucky you weren't home," he said. "The police were here looking for your husband and they wanted to question you. They think he might be a spy."

He went on. "They will come back. If they find you here, they will take you in for questioning and discover where your husband is. It's not safe for you to be here anymore. This is serious. They told me that Becker is head of the British Intelligence here." Becker — the man in the fine hotel who called Papa to help his wife when she had an asthmatic attack.

The background to this was the sizable German population in the southern and eastern parts of Brazil. Between the wars, many

Germans had seen economic opportunity in Brazil and moved there. The British worried that Brazil might be persuaded to join the Axis group. Brazil had significant natural resources and would also provide an important strategic base for the Axis. There were also newspaper headlines about German submarines spotted off the coast of Brazil, raising concerns that the Nazis were dropping off agents or possibly receiving supplies from Nazi sympathizers. Thus the British were indeed conducting intelligence operations in Brazil. Papa's contact with Becker raised the suspicions of the Brazilian police.

Roberto continued, "In fact, the English have already bundled Becker off on a plane to England. The big guys always get away. Instead, they arrested the two boys that worked for him in the South. Now they are looking for your husband and they are serious about finding him."

Mutti straightened up and spoke strongly, "My husband is not a spy. That is just a misunderstanding. I will go right to the police station and clear it up."

Roberto looked dubious. He asked, "Has your visa expired?"

Mutti looked down and said softly, "Yes, several months ago." Then she added more firmly, "But we are registered with the Office for Registration of Foreigners. We believe that we should be able to get a *permanencia* [the right to remain indefinitely], because the office that issues permanencias was closed for repairs for a long time."

Papa did finally get a permanencia in September of the following year. Our original visitor's visa had expired in July of 1939 and until receipt of the permanencia in September of 1940 we were in Brazil without the right to remain. I remember my mother saying that whenever strangers appeared in Barra, she looked carefully at them to see if they were from the police. In trying to secure a permanencia, my father nearly lost his passport. He left it at the agency that issued permanencias and when he returned to check on progress, he was told that his passport had been mislaid and he should return yet again. Instead, he approached another clerk and used his knowledge of Brazilians' penchant for gambling to bet the clerk that the passport was in an upper drawer. The clerk accepted the bet and found the passport in that drawer.

"Please think carefully, Mrs. Weiser," said Roberto. "You want to go into the police station when you have overstayed your visa. I don't think going there is wise, especially now that they believe that your husband is a spy."

"But he's not a spy," Mutti moaned, near tears. "What am I supposed to do?"

"You have to leave this house right away," he said, "so the police won't find you here when they come back, as they certainly will."

"But where can we go?" Mutti asked, almost in despair. She pulled Lisl and me closer. I could feel her tension and was frightened at the thought of being evicted from our house.

"You are going to go to the boarding house across the street. I've already talked with them," Roberto said reassuringly. "The owner there is another immigrant and knows your husband. Grab your valuables and your children and go over right now. They are expecting you. The other women in the house will pack up your stuff so we can honestly say you left."

Mutti ran up the front steps and into our room. She took a string shopping bag, opened the nightstand drawer and put our passports, some other papers and a few valuables into the bag. She left the rest for the ladies to pack. Taking Lisl's hand and mine, she led us across the street. It was all happening fast. I had heard the landlord and Mutti talking but I was still confused.

"Where are we going? Why are we leaving again?" I asked. "Does Papa know where we're going? How will he find us?" Frowning and grumbling, I moved quickly to keep up with my mother.

When we arrived at the new boarding house, we didn't even

have to knock. The door swung open just as we got there and a smiling, stocky European woman greeted us with open arms, introducing herself as Miriam. She said that Papa had treated her husband when he was sick. They were not able to pay him and so were happy to pay that debt by letting us stay there. Mutti was overwhelmed by the welcome. And I was happy to hear another good thing Papa had done. Mutti smiled and hugged Miriam. She was humming as we walked up the stairs to our new room. It was a bright room with a large window looking down to a small garden beside the house. There were two good beds.

Mutti hugged us both and said, "I knew Papa would take care of us. We were just about out of money but Papa's good work paid our rent in advance. He is a good man." We stayed in a warm embrace for a few minutes.

A Sudden Departure

Having just settled into our new home (our fourth in Rio), we were on our way to breakfast one morning when Mutti was called to the house telephone. That was a very rare occurrence. She hurried to the phone and Lisl and I moved quickly to follow her. She took the phone and said, "Hello." Then she stood a little straighter. "Yes, Baroness," she said. I paid closer attention.

Mutti listened; she began to look worried. "But I have lessons scheduled and the children are going to school," I heard her say. Mutti was silent, now looking even more concerned. She stuttered "but, but" several times and then said, "Yes, Baroness, I will give you the telephone numbers of the schools and of my students."

"Can you tell me again when the train leaves?" She listened and said, "Yes, Baroness. Of course. We will make the train. Thank you, Baroness."

"Hurry, children!" she said as she hugged us. "We are going right now to see Papa and we have to rush to make the train."

I was thrilled at the prospect of seeing Papa after four months of separation beginning when he went to Barra. Then another thought occurred to me. "But, Mutti, I have school today, and if we leave, I would have to say goodbye to Father Alphonso and Dona Teresinha."

Mutti looked at me for a moment and then said, "I'm sorry, Hansi. The baroness is going to call your school and explain that we had to rush to Barra. The baroness is leaving tomorrow and we have to take care of her daughter. The administrative manager's wife got sick and can't make it. It's an emergency. You can write Father Alphonso and Dona Teresinha a letter. I am sure they will understand."

I was really upset. We had just been abruptly moved out of one place to another and now we were going to be moved again. I was really mad at the baroness, who had caused this. "Boy, she really orders people around, doesn't she?" I said, near tears. Mutti put her arm around me. "I'm sorry, Hansi," she said. "Let's look at the bright side. We are going to go to Papa and I think we'll just stay there with him in Barra."

It was only minutes later that we were saying our goodbyes and, clutching just two shopping bags, heading for the trolley that would take us to the station.

"Do you have money for the train tickets?" I asked my mother.

"No," she said, "but the baroness has arranged for a man to meet us at the station and give us our tickets."

"Boy, she does everything," I said.

"Think of the good things," Mutti advised.

She was right. I was mad at the baroness for upsetting things for me and making me leave without saying goodbye to Father Alphonso and Dona Teresinha. But then I thought about seeing Papa and about riding on the trolley and the train, which I always enjoyed. Now I'd have a chance to see new scenery on the train ride to Barra. I began to settle down. I still felt angry about having to leave Father Alphonso and Dona Teresinha without being able to say goodbye.

I asked my mother for paper and a pencil so I could write Father Alphonso. It was not easy because the trolley was rocking but I wrote slowly and carefully.

"Dear Father Alphonso, we are going to Barra, where my father is working. I am very sorry I did not have a chance to say goodbye to you and Dona Teresinha. Baroness Kummer was very pushy. I will miss you very much. Devotedly yours in Christ, João Weiser." ("João" is the Brazilian form of Johann.) I showed the letter to my mother. She said, "That's good."

After a moment, she asked, "Aren't you being a little hard on Baroness Kummer?"

I looked at the letter again and thought about it. Then I added, "PS Baroness Kummer is not a bad person. She was just in a hurry, Devotedly yours in Christ, João Weiser."

As the trolley rolled along, I looked at the people walking on the sidewalks and kids scooting around slow-walking pedestrians and the fruits and vegetables on display in the open-air shops. The activity on the streets soon had my full attention and I forgot my anger.

And then Mutti said, "Okay, get ready. The next stop is the train station."

3

INTO THE BACKCOUNTRY

Traveling to Barra

I t was February 1940 and we were on our way into the backcountry of Brazil after a year in Rio. We rumbled through industrial
areas, past warehouses, commercial structures and tracks leading
off in various directions. The clickety-clack settled in and we were
soon rolling through open country, with banana trees flitting by.
Lisl pointed out a rooster on a small hill waving his wings, "just
like in Hungary."

Mutti turned to us and asked, "Do you remember Grandmother's
white geese all marching in a row?"

I answered, "Yes, and the turkey with the red skin dangling
from his beak." I thought for a moment of the farmhouses in Hungary with long strings of red peppers and of yellow corn hanging
from the eaves. And the fruit trees with bright, fresh fruit. And the
well-maintained stone houses with neat gardens in the back facing the railroad tracks. And beyond the houses, the large, open,
flat fields of vegetables or grains. Outside the window, the countryside was different from Hungary. That neat, cultivated look was
replaced by open, scraggly fields surrounded by thick, lush bushes, trees and vines, punctuated by splashes of bright color from a
bougainvillea. Sometimes a large, wide-winged bird would rise
from the scrubby open fields. I enjoyed watching the countryside
flowing by. I enjoyed thinking about the people who lived in the
houses or the children who played in the yards or even how the

animals found their way to a shady spot at midday. Like my mother, who was very good at making up stories, I also tended to imagine events around the people and things I saw.

The train settled into a regular rhythm; many passengers nodded off and I felt a little drowsy myself. But then the train would slow and the change would rouse me. Several times we stopped at small stations. Once some boys came by the train selling fruit. Mutti bought two bananas and two oranges. At the stations, some passengers would step off and others would get on — local people carrying large, round bags, a few with luggage, and the women almost always wearing bright-colored clothes.

Once I saw a priest leaving the train and that made me think of Father Alphonso. He really was a good friend and I would miss him, as well as Dona Teresinha. And I had just been getting to know the other boys and beginning to feel less an outsider. And I had liked living in our house, just a half-block from the beach. I looked forward to being with Papa, but I wondered what it was going to be like in the place we would be living now. I had no idea what to expect.

I missed my Hungarian grandmother. I missed both my grandmothers. They were different from each other but I always knew they loved me. In fact, I missed Vienna and the park and my cousins and Hungary and Neni the cook and my small garden at the edge of Grandma Paula's lawn. But we were heading to yet another new place.

The train rumbled along and I looked at my mother. She was staring out the window but I don't think she was really looking. She was thinking, and periodically she'd straighten her dress. I suppose that like me she was thinking about what life would be like in Barra. She had always said that she wanted to be with Papa and I knew that was the most important thing for her. But I wasn't really sure what was going to happen to us.

Lisl, of course, had already befriended the other women passengers, who all wanted to hug her. She eventually ended up sitting
on the lap of a large black woman who sat opposite Mutti and fell
asleep there.

Five hours after we'd left Rio, the train began to slow down and
pulled into Campos, the large town where we were to get off. Mutti
told us someone would meet us and drive us to Barra.

We stepped off the train and walked to the center of the platform. We were not hard to spot — a white European woman with
two children wearing European clothes. Sure enough, a tall, thin
black man with a floppy hat and loose work clothes came toward
us. He gave us a big smile and said, "Hello, my name is Tiburcio.
The boss asked me to meet you and bring you to him in Barra. The
car is just over there." He pointed to the other side of the tracks and
there stood an old, mud-spattered car.

I looked at the man and asked, "Do you know Dr. Weiser? He
is my father."

"Oh, yes, I know him. He is my boss. He is a very good man,"
Tiburcio answered, smiling. I liked Tiburcio right away.

"Thank you for coming to pick us up, Mister Tiburcio," Mutti
said. "How far is it to Barra?"

"About eighty kilometers," Tiburcio answered.

"So we should be there in a couple of hours," Mutti said.

"That depends," Tiburcio answered, looking at a darkening sky.
Large heavy clouds were gathering in the west, starting to cover the
afternoon sun.

We took a dirt road out of town. The houses in Campos were
smaller than in Rio, but they were city houses, made of stone or
plaster. As we drove out into the country, we began to see houses
with thatched roofs and sides that looked like dried mud. There
were rough openings in the walls that served as windows but had
no glass in them. The houses were usually square and seemed to

have one or two rooms at most.

Tiburcio explained that the houses were made of mud and thatch. "You plant four poles for the corners, then you put smaller poles in the ground where the walls will be, and weave branches or saplings between and through the poles to make a mesh, and finally cover the mesh with mud. When the mud dries you have a wall that keeps out the wind and the rain. Everybody can make their own house."

Sometimes you'd see little children playing on the packed earth in front, some wearing a light shirt or short pants and some very young children wearing nothing. Most were barefoot. We didn't see any houses like the boarding houses where we lived in Rio. Often you'd see women leaning out of the window-openings, watching us drive by. These women looked nothing like the robust, apple-cheeked farm women I remembered from Hungary. Instead, they were thin and hollow-cheeked with mulatto coloring.

It was hot. I said so to Mutti and she said, "Yes, it's hot, but we shouldn't mind. The sun shines for everyone." That was an old Brazilian saying. Hearing it, Tiburcio chimed in, "Yes, the sun shines for all. He shines on every tree, bush and flower, and makes no

A view of the harbor in Barra.

difference between rich and poor." He laughed a contented laugh.

Mutti turned to me and said, "We're needed in Barra. We are like pioneers, helping to open up a new part of the country."

"But will we be able to stay?" I asked, thinking of our departure from Rio and of our several other departures in the last year.

"Of course. There is a lot of activity there because it's a place where a river runs into the sea. The farmers from up in the country come down the river with their produce; the fishermen come in with their catch. And now there will be a new factory there. It will be a place for us to stay," she explained.

We were quiet. Then Mutti saw my lips moving. "Did you say something?" she asked.

"No, I was just praying that we would stay," I said.

The road entered dark woods, which provided welcome shade but seemed eerie. There was dense growth; vines climbed up the trees and the undergrowth seemed impenetrable. It was not like the pine forests near Vienna where we sometimes went for a walk. There the woods seemed open and inviting, with little undergrowth between the trees. These woods seemed more scary and forbidding.

We bounced along. The long day on the train and the warm afternoon soon had Lisl and me nodding off. I think I might have slept nearly the whole way, despite the bouncing. I woke up when my arm felt wet. Mutti was pulling us closer as heavy rain came pouring down. Tiburcio was driving slowly and swerving left or right to avoid huge puddles.

Then I could hear rushing water. Tiburcio stopped the car. Ahead of us a short bridge spanned a creek, now rushing with white water from the downpour. Something was wrong on the bridge — a gap in the roadway. Tiburcio put on a short slicker and stepped out into the rain. He was going to get very wet. He walked slowly up to the bridge, examined it and walked carefully onto it. He stooped down and tugged on a large board, slowly repositioning it to lie parallel with the other boards in the roadway. He examined the result and, satisfied, returned to the car. He drove slowly across the bridge.

The rain lightened but left large puddles on the road. Tiburcio continued his slow, careful driving as he navigated the hazards. We left the woods and were again driving by open fields. The sun sank lower in the sky and shadows lengthened. We had been on the road for almost three hours. "Will we be there soon?" Mutti asked. "Oh, yes, it's coming," Tiburcio replied, laughing.

We drove on. A half hour later, we began to see clusters of huts along the road. The rain had stopped and people were coming out of their huts to check on the impact of the downpour. They waved as the car rolled by.

A man was walking beside the road. Tiburcio hailed him, stopped the car and got out. The two men chatted for several minutes. Mutti was getting anxious. She asked, "Is this Barra?"

"No," Tiburcio replied, laughing. "But we are getting near."

We started off again but we slowed regularly as Tiburcio waved to people standing by their huts or near the road. Sometimes he'd stop the car for a quick word. He seemed to know everyone and they all seemed happy to see him; many looked at us with friendly interest. When Tiburcio stopped again at a cluster of huts and jumped out to say something to another man, my mother asked anxiously, "Are we in Barra yet?"

"Yes, but we have a little bit further to go to get to the baron's house. We will be there in a few minutes." Tiburcio came back and we drove on.

As dusk was setting in, we began catching sight of water through the breaks in the shrubs alongside the road. It was a river, as wide as the four-lane avenue by Ipanema beach. It shimmered in the twilight.

The road turned sharply away from the river but instead of fol-

Baroness Kummer at the side door of her home.

lowing the road, Tiburcio drove straight ahead on a smaller dirt track. There, facing the track, stood a large, rectangular house. It was solid, sturdy and well maintained. An open yard and a flower garden stood beside it. Stone steps led from the yard into the house.

"That is the baron's house," announced Tiburcio. "We are here."

Papa came bouncing down the steps of the house. He raced to the car and gave Mutti a long hug. Then he picked up Lisl, kissing her on the cheek, and bent down and kissed me on my cheek, tousling my hair. I grabbed his hand and held it tightly. "I am so happy to have you all here," he exclaimed joyfully. He led us up the stairs into the house.

We entered a long hallway with doors along either side. He led Lisl and me into one room and then Mutti into the one next door. Each had a double bed, a bureau and a curtained window looking out onto the yard.

We cleaned up and went in to dinner.

Four people were sitting at a large rectangular table. Light came from candles on the table in crystal holders and two kerosene lamps on a mantel to the side. The baroness sat at the head of the table. Next to her was a distinguished-looking gentleman dressed in crisp riding pants and a white shirt who rose as we entered. This was Kolszinski, whom Mutti had met at the Burjans' house in Rio. A tall, thin man also rose and introduced himself as Franzen, the accountant for the plant. Finally, there was Elfriede Maria, the daughter of the baron and baroness, called Marie. They all welcomed us and we sat down. There was plenty of room — the table could seat more than a dozen people.

A tall black man entered wearing white gloves and carrying a large serving platter. On it was a whole cooked fish. I am not sure I had ever seen one served that way and, as hungry as I was, it stopped me for a moment. Lisl looked as uncertain as I did. The server, whose name was Matthias, put the platter down next to the baroness and delicately cut the fish and removed its meat from the bones. After offering the platter to the baroness, he offered it to Marie, who took a piece. Next he served Mutti. She took a large piece and cut two smaller portions from it. She asked Lisl and me to pass our plates to her, and put a small piece on each of our plates. I took a small bite and it tasted good. I ate it all. After we finished dinner, Mutti had Lisl and me say goodnight to the adults and took us off to our room to go to bed.

Getting Settled in Barra

Lisl and I slept soundly; Mutti had to wake us for breakfast. The baroness had already left and Papa had gone out earlier to review the progress of the construction work. Mutti was laughing when she told us, "Papa and I got up early, put on our bathing suits and gave each other a shower with the watering can because the shower in the guest bathroom isn't connected yet. It was fun. Maybe we'll do you later."

We sat at the kitchen table and Mutti made Lisl and me each an egg and gave us bread and jam. We ate it hungrily. Just as we were finishing, Papa came in and said, "Why don't I take you all for a walk around, so you can see what is happening here. You'll enjoy it." Now, we would get our first glimpse of the plant that Papa had been working on and the reason why we were here.

As we stepped out of the door, the river caught my eye. It was right there, just across the dirt path, flowing by the house, strong and quiet and beautiful in the sunlight.

A clattering sound behind me made me turn around. And there stood a huge boxy building, many times the size of the baron's house. A tall brick chimney next to the building rose into the sky. And I could glimpse other structures behind the main building. Trucks were driving in and out, and men were moving in all directions. It was a beehive of activity. Wow! So this is what Papa is working on, I thought.

*The baron checks plans during construction of
the tapioca factory in Barra.*

Papa held my hand and Mutti held Lisl's as we walked toward
the big building. "Let me show you how you make tapioca flour,"
Papa said.

As we walked, Papa said, "Once the buildings were up, we put
the machinery inside. Now we are testing to make sure it all works.
In a few weeks the plant will be ready for formal commissioning.
Let me show you the cassava root we use to make tapioca."

We walked to a large pile of roots, orange brown in color, with a
rough skin, the size of large yams. Papa picked up one of them and
said, "These grow in the ground like potatoes; farmers dig them up
and put them in our trucks, which bring them here. We peel the
roots and feed them into a slicer that cuts them into small pieces.
A furnace then dries the pieces and the mill grinds the dry pieces
into flour."

Papa pointed out the building where the cutting machinery
would be installed and the long shed where the cut pieces of root
would be dried. He called it the *seccador*, meaning "dryer" in Portuguese. The mill was a big building in the center of the plant. As we
stood there, we had a chance to greet Tiburcio, who was unloading
boxes from a truck. Papa had appointed him foreman of the plant.

Walking back to the house, Papa stopped by another man whom he introduced as Senhor Vargas. He looked different from Tiburcio. Tiburcio was black, tall and thin. You could see his muscles ripple. Vargas was olive-skinned, obviously strong but chunkier. In Rio, Mutti often remarked on the wide range of appearance of the people in Brazil — there were blacks who were almost ebony in color, as well as a range of mulattos with skin tones that approached coffee with milk, to almost white. There were people with light skins, like those of us from Austria and Germany, and people of Mediterranean descent, including Portuguese and Egyptians, who had more olive-colored skin and strong features.

A focal point of the landscape was a water tank that the baron had built. It was well over two stories high, with a deck at mid-level. A railing ran around the outside of the deck. You had to climb carefully up a long metal ladder, hand over hand, to make your way up. Papa took Mutti up there the day after we arrived to give her a better sense of the lay of the land. When they returned, Mutti said, "There is a beautiful view from there. You can see the ocean, the village and some farms when you look toward the mountains. I really enjoyed it."

Papa told us that the water tank held water for the plant and for the baron's house. Because the water tank was up high, water would rush out of a faucet when you opened it. That was important if there was a fire and you needed water to put out the fire. It also made water flow in the baron's house for the showers and the toilets.

I think only the few houses built by the baron had toilets; most people had outhouses. There was no municipal water system or sewer system. People got water from the river to wash and cook. Drinking water had to be brought from Boa Sorte, a village nearby that had a spring with clean, fresh water.

The next afternoon Papa came and said, "Let's go up the water tank."

"Wonderful," I said and gave him a hug.

Papa took me to the deck, where you had a beautiful view. As Mutti had said, I saw the ocean; and in the other direction open land and fazendas stretched to the mountains. You could also see the road that ran by the pharmacy and follow it until it disappeared into the distance.

I really liked looking down and seeing the roofs of the village — the baron's house, the schoolhouse and the houses and huts of the villagers. I've always enjoyed seeing things from above. Even today I prefer the window seat on an airplane, so I can look down on the farms and villages and cities and imagine the people below, leading their lives and going about their chores.

That evening, as we sat down for dinner, I looked around the room and saw a radio on one of the shelves. I was excited because it gave me an idea.

I kept an eye on Kolszinski's wristwatch. As the minute hand reached twelve, I got up and moved to the radio. I turned it on, knowing that at seven o'clock every night, the radio played the national anthem of Brazil. I turned the volume up and stood at attention as the music poured out. Papa said, "Hansi, please turn that down." I answered, "But this is the anthem of our country, of our nation. We should listen to it and honor it."

Papa came over and turned off the radio and told me to sit down. I was glad I'd had the chance to hear the national anthem. We all need a country, I thought. Still, I think Papa and Mutti were not happy with what I did. I was sorry about that. I did not want to create a bad impression, but hearing the national anthem always moved me and I loved to hear it every chance I got.

One of the first places Mutti took Lisl and me was to the bachelors' house to introduce ourselves to other Europeans who worked at the plant. The house was next door to the baron's house, a short walk under tall palm trees. A simple, one-story structure larger

Papa, Enrique, Paolo, Lotte, Franzen and Mutti in front of the bachelors' quarters. The water tower appears to the left.

than other houses in Barra, it had four bedrooms, a kitchen and a living room. It was one of the four houses the baron had built: his own house, the schoolhouse, the bachelors' quarters, and the guest house for business visitors.

Three men lived in the bachelors' quarters: Franzen, the accountant we had met at dinner at the baron's house, Enrique, the administrative manager, and Paolo, the engineering manager. Mutti said later that you could tell that men lived there because clothes were lying around and dishes lay piled in the sink. After we introduced ourselves, blue-eyed Enrique said, "Try to stay at the baron's house as long as you can. Those rich people treat their guests well. It's really different when you are living on your own. We cook for ourselves and we have to get our own provisions, which is not easy since a lot of things have to be brought in from Campos."

All three men were emigrants from Europe. Franzen was from Germany, Enrique from France and Paolo from Italy. Later, we learned that Paolo had been living in Austria and was also a refugee.

Papa and the Plant

The construction of the mill was finished in early January, more than a month before Mutti, Lisl and I arrived in Barra. The baron allowed almost two months of start-up operations to make sure all was working well and then set the commissioning of the plant for March of 1940. He made it into a big event. He managed to attract dignitaries from the government, including the daughter of the president of Brazil, Getúlio Vargas, and her husband, a senior government official, who are pictured in the photo opposite. They in turn brought their own entourage, so altogether there must have been thirty distinguished visitors present. Most of the plant workers and other villagers stood on the sidelines looking on. Speeches were exchanged, flags were raised, and guests toured the facilities. The picture shows several very tall men, well over six feet. It also shows two boys, one on either side of the crowd. One of them looks like me.

The presence of those dignitaries, far from their comfortable offices in Rio, gives some sense of the baron's influence and perhaps the importance of a new mill in the backcountry. These people made the long journey to what they must have considered a godforsaken place. But it was the opening of a significant industrial venture deep in rural country.

The plant made a successful trial run. It met the completion requirements and was handed over to the baron and his team. Papa

Baron Kummer, left, with the daughter of Brazil's President Getúlio Vargas and her husband during the inauguration of the tapioca plant in Barra.

remained a key player on that team. The baron was now even more committed to selling plant output. And selling that tapioca had to be done in Rio and São Paulo, so the baron spent weeks on the road. That left Kolszinski and Papa as the senior men in charge. Kolszinski trusted Papa and was happy to leave supervision of operations to him. There was, however, one problem.

The evening after the baron left, I heard Papa say to Mutti, "The baron said that the mill was to operate seven days a week. I asked him to reconsider and give the men one day off a week to rest. But he said no, the plant did not need a day of rest, we needed the income and it was more economical to run the plant all the time rather than starting and stopping it. He may be right about the plant but not about the men. I am going to have to find a way to organize shifts so the men can have some time off."

As I learned, you had to train a lot of people to run a tapioca mill. In the weeks before the plant was completed, the baron, Kolszinski, Papa, Tiburcio and others prepared and reviewed plans for how the plant would operate, where men would be stationed and what they were expected to do. The men who were going to work in the plant were locals without any experience of operating machinery or the milling process. So a lot of training was needed: explanations of how the machines worked, what their duties would be, and safety warnings.

Papa had been at the plant for five months by the time it was commissioned and he had used the time to learn as much as he could about it. He felt reasonably prepared as operations commenced. He also used the time to get to know the men who had been hired and would continue when the plant began operations. They included the two Europeans, Paolo and Enrique, as well as Tiburcio and Vargas, whom Papa had appointed as foreman and assistant foreman. There was another Brazilian as well, Alfredinho.

Alfredinho was from Campos and had experience with machinery. Only he and Paolo had such experience. While neither had worked with machinery at a tapioca mill, they could use their general knowledge to diagnose anything that might have gone wrong at the mill and work toward an answer. Papa relied on both of them.

Papa's main work was to help the men, inexperienced as they were, to meet their assignments and deal with the problems that predictably arose in a new system. He relied on Tiburcio and Vargas, who had an easy, natural authority with the villagers, to work with them more directly.

Sometimes Papa contributed his own ingenuity to the operation of the plant. One day, Papa came into the kitchen of the baron's house, drenched with sweat and with grime on his clothes. He got a glass of water, drank it all down and then sat for a moment. He seemed exhausted. A few minutes later, Kolszinski came in. "Why is the plant shut down?" he asked.

Papa said, "We've had recurring problems with small pieces of the cutting equipment breaking off and then tearing the screens used to filter out lumps in the flour. We've regularly had to shut the line down to repair the screens. I think I've figured out a way to fix the problem."

"What is your solution?" Kolszinski asked.

"I've set up some magnets on the line before the screens," Papa said. "They should attract and hold any metal fragments before they hit the screens. And the magnets should be relatively easy to clean. It means that we won't have to stop the plant so often."

"That is marvelous! Excellent idea, Arthur, thank you," Kolszinski said. He left the house smiling.

I learned about another of Papa's ideas another day when Kolszinski stopped by the lab. He saw some equipment and asked what it was. Papa replied, "It's some experimental equipment I've been building with the idea of making alcohol or ethanol from cassava. I've read that it's been done in labs and I hope we might eventually make it on a commercial basis. It could provide another source of income and be insurance if our quota for flour is cut. And we have all the cassava we could want." Kolszinski agreed. "That is a great idea. Let me know how you progress."

A major event at the plant involved the arrival of a tractor. It started when Kolszinski received a telegram one night at dinner. He opened it while at the dinner table and his face darkened. He said to my father, "The baron has purchased a new tractor for almost 75,000 cruzeiros. It is a big gamble. Excuse me, please. I'm afraid I won't be able to eat the rest of my dinner. I have lost my appetite." He left the table and the dinner conversation stopped.

That evening, as my parents were putting us to bed, Mutti asked Papa about Kolszinski's behavior at dinner.

Papa said, "Kolszinski is not happy about the expenditures. He is worried about the budget for the project, and as a partner he is also worried that his share of the venture will be diluted because his funds are very limited."

It was only a week after the telegram came that the tractor arrived by ship. The ship was itself new, having been built at the

The ship commissioned by the Baron decked out with festive flags.

shipyard just up the road from the baron's house and launched four weeks before it brought the tractor. Papa told us that the launch had been a gala event. Everyone in the village had come, many in their Sunday best. The ship, over 100 feet long, looked enormous as it loomed above the crowd on the shipbuilding ramps. With the cabin on top, it must have been three stories high and was fitted with large masts in front and back. For the launch, men at the shipyard had hung colorful flags from the bow to the top of the front mast across to the back mast and then down to the stern, giving the occasion a festive air.

Then the baron strode onto the scene. The crowd parted and opened a path for him to walk up to the ship. The master of the shipyard handed him a large sledge hammer. As the spectators held their breath, the baron, with one determined swing, dislodged a large wooden beam that was jammed between the stern of the ship and the ground. He moved out of the way as shipyard hands on either side of the ship dislodged other blocks and untied lines. Slowly the ship slid down the ramps and into the water. It settled into the river and rocked gently. A loud cheer rose from the crowd. A big

The baron on the gangplank of the ship he commissioned.

smile spread across the baron's face. Later, when a gangplank was set up, he walked up to the ship.

I was sorry to have missed seeing the launch. It must have been thrilling.

Another piece of the baron's plan, the ship was going to haul flour from the mill to markets in Rio. It could carry many more sacks of flour than trucks, and travel by water avoided the long and sometimes difficult drive into Campos and the process of unloading the flour from trucks and then loading it onto railroad cars. The ship also provided an alternate way for people to travel to and from Rio. It often returned from Rio with one or more new employees, and Mutti used it to take an overnight trip to Rio.

The ship was on a two-week cycle. Every time it arrived, there was something new to be seen. It was a wonderful break in the routine. There were no movies in the village and few radios, and TVs were a long way into the future, so the ship's arrival provided entertainment in real time. The arrivals were always festive, social

Workers loading tapioca sacks onto a ship at the dock.

occasions. Many of the villagers came and the young girls primped and put flowers in their hair. You never knew what the ship was going to bring.

The day the tractor arrived, Mutti, Lisl and I were part of the crowd. People expected the tractor be lifted off the ship and deposited on the dock using the boom on the ship's deck, just the way deckhands unloaded other cargo. However, because the tractor was large and heavy, the ship hands and the men in the shipyard decided on a different approach. The ship's arrival was timed to coincide with low tide, so the deck would be close to the height of the dock. The shipyard crane laid a series of large beams side by side from the deck of the ship directly onto the dock; they were tied together with a heavy rope to form a strong gangway.

The lines were untied, the shrouding canvas lifted and the tractor revealed. It was a handsome piece of machinery. One of the crew slowly drove it down the temporary gangway, turned off the engine and set the brake. Then he handed the keys to Papa, who was the senior project man present.

Papa walked around the tractor, examining it with a gleam in his eye. He appreciated a fine piece of machinery. He had spent many summers at his grandfather's farm, so he knew a good tractor when he saw one. And his years serving in the Hungarian army during the First World War also served to instill an appreciation for good working machinery. He knew that good machinery deserved good care. It earned its keep.

Papa ran his hand carefully over the hood of the new tractor, looked at the crowd and tugged his earlobe — giving the Brazilian sign that something was really good. The villagers laughed in delight.

Then Papa turned his attention to Paolo, who had been standing next to Papa, shifting restlessly from foot to foot. Paolo was a handsome fellow, with a Roman profile, high cheekbones, a full head of black hair and a well-muscled body. A scar that ran down one side of his face gave him a rakish air. Hired for his experience with machines, he was anxious to get his hands on the wheel of the tractor and to feel the throb of power under him. Now Papa handed him the keys. He climbed aboard the tractor as the young girls looked on admiringly. Papa advised him to go cautiously.

Paolo nodded yes, revved the engine, released the brake and headed slowly for the field, the crowd scattering to get out of his way. Paolo sat high and erect, like a captain on a horse.

In Kolszinski's car Papa headed after Paolo and the tractor, followed by a truck. Mutti, Lisl and I walked from the dock to the rise above the field to watch. From there, we could see the tractor move steadily down the long field. Then it turned and came back, clearing the ground of brush and undergrowth. At the near end of the field, it turned again and headed once more to the far end, working in a systematic way. It returned and began heading to the far end again for a third pass. But this time, the tractor seemed to be picking up speed. Paolo's nostrils flared; he sat even taller; the engine revved faster.

Papa was waving his arms and yelling for Paolo to slow down

but the roar of the tractor engine drowned Papa's warning and Paolo was not looking back. Now the car sped along the field chasing after the tractor but Paolo only looked ahead. The tractor hurtled toward the end of the field, which merged into a swamp. Paolo seemed mesmerized. The tractor continued at full tilt. Then, frighteningly, its nose dipped. As it moved further into the soft ground, it began to sink ever so slowly and ever so steadily into the swamp. The front wheels sank out of view and the nose tilted dangerously. The whole tractor was at a precarious angle. Paolo seemed unable to do anything.

Papa grabbed a rope from the back of the truck and threw it toward Paolo. Landing across Paolo's back, the rope startled him into action. He tied the rope to the tractor and, hand over hand, made his way back from the swamp, toward the car. Kolszinski lit a cigarette with quiet deliberation and handed it to Paolo. Paolo dragged on it deeply.

Papa tied the other end of the rope to the axle of the truck, had the driver back up slowly, and got some men who were standing around watching to push against the truck. The rope tightened, the men pushed, the truck revved, but the tractor barely moved before the truck wheels started slipping. "What can we do?" Kolszinski asked.

Papa thought a moment and then asked the men to round up a half dozen pair of oxen with their yokes. Those of us on the rise looked sadly at the beautiful tractor half sunk in the ooze. Would it be a total loss? Would it ever work again?

An hour later, enough oxen had arrived. In the meantime, Papa had collected some more rope. He had the men line the six pair of oxen one pair behind the other and ran ropes from each yoke back to the tractor. Once it was all connected, Papa had the men goad the oxen forward. They moved steadily until the ropes tightened. We onlookers held our breath. There was a momentary pause, but while some oxen's feet slipped, enough had traction, and as they pushed and pushed again against their yokes, the tractor shuddered and slowly began to rise from the mud. It was like a rebirth. We cheered.

Finally, the tractor stood on solid ground with mud oozing off all over it. Paolo jumped aboard and tried to start the engine. Nothing happened. Those of us on the hill feared the worst. The machine had drowned. The body had been rescued but life was gone. But Papa said that once the parts had been cleaned of the mud and greased, it should be fine.

So in their reliable, old-fashioned way, the oxen dragged the fancy new machine up the road to the repair shop. Papa organized a bucket brigade to bring water from the river and rinse off the tractor. The coat of mud slid off and the bright red of the finish reappeared. It took two days for the engine to be disassembled, cleaned, greased and put back together. It was running well when the baron returned from his trip. Just as well. It was easier to forgive and forget as Paolo drove the tractor on its assignments.

A cart pulled by a team of oxen like those that rescued the sinking tractor.

A Child Named Arthura

P apa was not licensed to practice medicine in Brazil. Yet, in the absence of other doctors or medical assistance in Barra, he was often asked to use his medical expertise.

There was one dramatic incident that did much to enhance Papa's reputation with the villagers. We had been in Barra a few weeks when one afternoon Mutti went looking for Papa. Vargas told her, "The pharmacist came by. He was in a hurry and asked the doc to go with him."

Mutti headed for the pharmacist's shop, which actually carried general goods — nails in barrels, bolts of cloth and other dry goods — in addition to bottles of medicines. I followed.

The pharmacist, Aristides Ribeiros de Santiago, owned several parcels of land and was the undisputed leader of the village. Just arriving astride a thin, small horse, he wore a smudged shirt, dusty pants and a worn wide-brimmed straw hat. He slid off the horse, picked up a piece of wood and scraped the mud off the soles of his bare feet.

Excusing herself to the women waiting in line, Mutti pushed forward to speak with the pharmacist. He saw her but motioned for her to wait while he examined a rash on a man's chest. Satisfied with the exam, Ribeiros made a notation in a notebook and gave the man a bottle with dark pills. Then he walked over to my mother, gave her a friendly *abraço* ("hug" in Portuguese) and asked, "Dona

Theresa, how can I help you?"

"Please, Senhor Ribeiros, I am looking for my husband. Vargas said you asked for him. Do you know where he is?"

"Oh, yes," Ribeiros said. "He is at Marta's house. She is having difficulty delivering a baby. In fact, it may be too late, but I thought the doc might be able to help her." He showed Mutti the way to Marta's house.

Several of the villagers standing by the pharmacy door heard Ribeiros' comment that it might be too late for Marta's baby and quickly dispersed to spread the news. Mutti took my hand. I had to jog to keep up with her. She seemed very concerned.

We came to a wall of large shrubs. The path led through an opening to a patch of packed red earth around six or eight simple mud huts with thatched roofs and ill-fitting wooden shutters rather than glass windows. The people's clothes were very worn, with ragged edges. A group of villagers stood outside one of the huts. I stepped inside with Mutti and we stopped a moment while our eyes adjusted to the darkness inside. We were in the living area of the hut. We could see a table, two benches and a cooking area in the corner. Five women were sitting at the table, some crying softly. On the table was a metal container with water and Papa's instruments. A low wall jutted out, separating the sleeping area. Over the wall, we saw a woman lying on a bed and another woman sitting almost astride the foot of the bed. Mutti led me outside and told me to wait. I decided to stand near the open door and listen.

A bit later, Mutti came out to see how I was doing. "Hansi, Papa is doing all he can," she said. "Just wait here and let's pray it all goes well." We heard a muffled scream from the hut and Mutti moved quickly back inside.

The scream unnerved me. For a few minutes all I could hear was some murmuring, then another scream — that gave me goose bumps. And then there was a happy shout, and then another, and then I heard, "The baby is alive!" The villagers outside embraced each other and danced with joy. The baby was alive! Relief and joy abounded.

When Mutti came out of the hut, she gave me a big hug and said, "Your Papa was wonderful. A new baby has been born and all is well with the mother." Papa looked very happy as he reached down and tousled my hair. Holding hands, we walked home together.

On the way, Mutti said, "The baby was a girl and in Brazil a girl is usually named after her mother, and then her first baby girl is usually named after her. And they do that for three generations. So we know there is going to be an Arthura in this village for many years."

"Arthura?" I asked.

"Yes," Mutti said. "Even though the new baby is a girl, she was named after Papa." When the baby girl was born, Papa had handed her to her mother. Marta cuddled her and then asked Papa to baptize her.

"What name would you like to call your daughter?" Papa asked Marta.

She said, "I'd like to name her after you."

Papa paused and said, "But my name is a man's name: Arthur."

The mother was not flustered. "That's fine. We'll call her 'Arthura,'" she declared.

Delivering Arthura and saving the tractor seemed to me to be really heroic acts by Papa. That gave me an idea. I found a piece of paper and a pencil and sat at the dining room table. I wrote, "Dear Father Alphonso, My father has saved a baby that many thought was dead and delivered it safely to its mother. And my father saved the life of the driver of a tractor who was frozen on the machine as it was sinking in the swamp and would have gone down with the tractor. And then my father saved the tractor itself which was worth thousands of cruzeiros as it was sinking in the swamp. They can't throw us out of Brazil now. Can they? Devotedly yours in Christ, João Weiser."

I asked Franzen for an envelope and he offered to address it for me. I answered, "I want to send it to my friend, Father Alphonso in Rio."

"Do you know Father Alphonso's address?" Franzen asked.

"Oh, I am sure that if it's addressed to Father Alphonso, the mailman will know him. He is known by a lot of people."

Franzen said. "Maybe I can ask your mother if she can add to the address, to make it easier for the postman."

I felt better as I left. When someone does the things Papa had done, they should really want to keep you.

That evening Mutti said that she had told Franzen that Father Alphonso was at Guy de Fontgalland school on Avenida Lago. She told me she thought that might help, just in case there was another Father Alphonso in Rio. That seemed unlikely to me but it was okay. She asked what I had written and I told her. She gave me a long hug and told me that it was a very good idea. She agreed that Papa was doing remarkable things and people should be aware of how big a contribution he was making. She admitted that she also sometimes worried about the government imprisoning us for overstaying our visa and that she always became anxious when a stranger rode into town, concerned about whether he was from the police. It would be a big relief, she said, if the government agreed with what I had written and let us stay. Maybe Father Alphonso could help after all.

I hoped I'd hear back from Father Alphonso soon.

Backcountry Life

One day in early April, the ship brought Lotte, Franzen's wife. There was the usual crowd to meet the ship, with Franzen in the front. As the ship docked, we could see a woman standing at the rail. She was thin, almost boyish-looking with dark hair cut short, strong features and an aquiline nose. She wore a neat white blouse and a long dark skirt. Once disembarked, she shared a long hug with Franzen. All the ladies looked at her closely and watched as the couple walked, hand in hand, to the house.

That afternoon, after Franzen went back to the office, Mutti took Lisl and me to meet Lotte. As we approached the bachelors' house, we overheard Enrique say to Paolo, "Why didn't Franzen tell us that he was bringing a scarecrow?"

Mutti said to us, "Those boys will be very happy to have a woman in the house, someone they can admire and someone to remind them of the women in their lives. Lotte will make their house more like a home."

Mutti knocked at Franzen's door. A woman's voice said, "Come in," and we entered. Lotte held some small nails between her lips while tapping the nails into fabric, covering a large box. Mutti introduced herself and us and asked what Lotte was doing.

"I'm making a vanity table," said Lotte.

"What are you going to use it for?" Mutti asked.

Sounding defensive, Lotte said, "I'm making it for myself. I'm a woman, aren't I?" A bottle with pink lotion, a small china dish with bobby pins, a brush and a comb stood on the table. She handed Mutti a long piece of fabric, pulled the chair next to the window and stood on it.

"Now hand me the top of the fabric, the part that's folded over," Lotte instructed and Mutti passed it up for Lotte to nail to the top of the window frame. The fabric softened the window and filtered the light coming in.

Mutti said, "That's a real improvement."

"Well," Lotte replied, "I have to dress it up the best I can. After all, this is my honeymoon suite."

Surprised, Mutti asked, "Haven't you been married? Haven't you lived together?'

Lotte said, "Nothing is simple any more. Franzen and I knew each other as youngsters in Germany and then our families fled to different countries, but Franzen and I wrote each other and then wrote more and we realized that we had become very fond of each other. Eventually he and I agreed that I would join him here. But my parents said I couldn't come unless we were married. Franzen and I agreed and were married by proxy."

Mutti said, "And you haven't seen your husband since the marriage?"

"Of course not," Lotte answered. "The baron is so cheap that he wouldn't let anyone travel unless it was on business. I told them Franzen needed me urgently. Just look at those bachelors. Each of them yearning for some girl he's lost or left somewhere. And that baroness, so refined and so mannered. I met her in Rio; she was as cold as her husband."

The front door opened and the tall, lanky Enrique sauntered in. "Hello," he said and let himself fall on the double bed, boots and all. Hands behind his head, he lay there and looked at us.

"Get off that bed and be sure that your boots don't dirty that cover," Lotte barked. "Sorry to spoil your fun, but this is my room now, mine and Franzen's, and don't walk in without knocking."

"Okay, okay, don't get so hissy," Enrique huffed as he walked out.

Now Lotte opened the door that led to the main room of the house. "Boy, if that isn't a mess, I don't know what is," she said, looking around the main room where clothes were scattered all around. A wash basin with dirty water stood on a chair. Water had stained the table and the floor in several spots. We looked into the other bedrooms. On one bed a mouse looked up quizzically. None of the beds were made but on the wall over each bed there was a shelf that held, almost altar-like, pictures of family with fresh-cut flowers by them. As we left, Lotte was standing there and looking at the scene with dismay.

The next day Mutti took Lisl and me on a walk with Lotte. We started by the baron's house. Lotte admired the solid structure. "It does remind you of Austria, doesn't it?" she asked.

I did not point out to Lotte the long, thin island a bit upstream. It always seemed dark and spooky to me. It was thick with dark trees. There was thick vegetation at ground level; vines climbed trees and snaked across to other trees. The island was barely above the level of the river and you sensed that it must be swampy. The island's saving grace was a flock of large white birds that roosted in the tree tops. Periodically, you'd hear the beating of wings and a cloud of white would rise into the sky.

Mutti led Lotte past the boatyard and the small cantina, whose pink paint was peeling badly. The cantina consisted of a large room, with a bar at the back. Open to the road, it contained a large table and some chairs.

The road followed the river and was lined by a dozen well-built houses, most of which had small gardens with rows of flowers or shrubs to mark property lines. In the months since we had arrived, Mutti had worked at meeting and befriending the local women.

Now they greeted her warmly and several, including Marianna Ribeiros, the pharmacist's wife, came out of their homes to meet Lotte. Lisl and I had visited the Ribeiroses' daughter at their home. The Ribeiroses' house was smaller than the baron's, of course, but it was much better than the hut I had visited when Papa delivered Arthura. The Ribeiroses had four rooms: two bedrooms, a living/dining room and a kitchen. The house was also made of stone. But mainly it was attractive because Dona Ribeiros was a warm, friendly woman and her little daughter Nelsa was a delight. Both Lisl and I enjoyed playing with her and she of course was delighted to have two playmates right in her house.

We reached the edge of an open field where Mutti told Lotte to close her eyes and listen. Lisl and I did the same. And so I heard birds singing — the shriek of the orioles, the peal of the bell birds, the broken sound of the *tapaculos* (gray, robin-sized birds with reddish throats) and the chirping of a flock of small birds whose names I did not know.

When we walked home, we stopped at Lotte's garden. Lotte

Donkey carrying a load of wood, a typical street scene in Barra in the early 1940s.

had started a garden next to the bachelors' house. I was allotted a small plot between Lotte's garden and the baroness' kitchen garden. I looked forward to having my own garden. I had enjoyed watching things grow at our cottage by the Danube in Austria and picking the strawberries that grew there.

Xixi, one of the local women, who was a good gardener, helped me plant some flowers. She told me the dark soil, the sun and the rain in Barra were good for plants. In fact, you had to work regularly to pull out the things you didn't want. I enjoyed kneeling on the ground and pulling weeds, and setting sticks to prop the plants I wanted to keep. Sometimes Lotte and I would work side by side.

One afternoon I needed a knife to sharpen some sticks to prop up plants. I went to ask if I could borrow Lotte's pocket knife. I hardly recognized her room. Lotte had painted the walls a light yellow and the floors a warm brown. She also painted the furniture. "Wow!" I said. "Sure looks nice." But Lotte looked like she had been crying.

"What's the matter, Lotte? Are you homesick?" I asked. "Were you thinking of things back home in Germany?"

She sat up on the bed and I went to her and took her hand. She put an arm around me and gave me a small hug. "Yes, I was," Lotte replied.

I looked at her for a moment and asked, "Did you have a Volksgarten, a people's park, in Berlin?"

"Yes," she said.

I looked toward the window and said quietly, "Sometimes we went to the Volksgarten very early in the morning, before other people were there. Then you'd hear the birds singing to each other. One would start, then others would reply, each with its own song."

Lotte answered, "And then the custodian would come and wipe down all the chairs and benches, hoping maybe for a tip."

"And our custodian had a hose that snaked around the park as he watered the flowers and plants," I added.

"Did your park have a Temple of Theseus, like ours?" I asked.

"No," she replied.

I said, "The custodian would dust off the feet of the statue outside the temple and once a week he'd wash the floor of the temple. We had a lot of fun playing around the statue and around the temple."

"Did the big boys help you?" Lotte asked.

"Oh, yes," I said, "Like they showed us how to build small sand castles using the wet dirt when the custodian watered. And when the Germans came, they were so excited and we all marched around like soldiers."

And then I fell silent as I remembered the empty feeling when the boys began to avoid me, when they behaved as if I wasn't even there, even including some that had been especially good friends of mine. I could never figure out quite why, but it hurt.

Lotte gave me another hug. "Well, some things we remember with pleasure; others are painful." She said. Then she gave me the pocket knife and I dashed out.

Some weeks later, Mutti and Lotte were out for a walk, which had become an almost daily routine. Mutti had always enjoyed walking and hiking. Of course, walking in Barra differed from mountain hiking in Austria. Still, both Mutti and Lotte enjoyed the exercise. Much as they enjoyed the walk, they enjoyed their chats even more, ranging over a broad set of topics, from local gossip, to family, to the homes they left behind in their escapes from Europe, and in Lotte's case, a deep yearning to return there. Mutti's focus was on the more immediate — her husband and her children.

The day was sunny, as usual. It was humid, as usual. It was hot, as usual, but not as hot as the day before, and there was a welcome breeze from the ocean. Palm fronds were swaying, an always welcome sign of a cooling ocean breeze. The ladies had settled into their rhythm. As they turned a corner, they saw Fritz ahead. Fritz, a young Austrian man with a pleasant, open face, had arrived a few weeks after Lotte to be Papa's new assistant.

When they met, Mutti said. "Well, now that you've been here while, what do you think?"

Fritz laughed. "When I realized there was no municipal sewer system, I realized that life would be different here than in Rio. The baron really sold me a bill of goods. He made it sound like I was coming to a country club, lovely beaches, attractive girls, easy living."

"What are you going to do?" Lotte asked.

"Grin and bear it," Fritz replied. "I enjoy working with Dr. Weiser and there's a lot to learn. And for foreigners like us, decent paying jobs are hard to find. I'll stay awhile."

Fritz had not been in Barra long when word spread that two priests were coming to Barra. That caused real excitement in the village. Sure enough, one day, a truck pulled up with two priests — and a surprise. An upright piano was roped carefully in the back of the truck. The priests drove the truck slowly toward the church as a crowd followed them. The priests asked two of the men looking on to help them move the piano into the church. Mutti arrived at the church just after the piano had been placed inside. She asked one of the priests if she might try playing it.

"Of course," he said. Mutti sat down and a dam broke. Months of no music and now her favorite instrument at her fingertips. She played as if in a trance. The church filled with music and she played on. She had a large repertoire memorized and she dove into it.

Word spread quickly around the village. None had ever heard a live performance by a concert-quality artist. Mutti had given many recitals as a young woman and she was enjoying herself now. No reason to be nervous about her performance here. She played on. A crowd collected; they were enchanted.

Half an hour later, Matthias the butler appeared next to her. With a solemn look, he asked, "Can you play 'Ave Maria'?"

"Yes," Mutti answered. She had barely begun to play the song when his beautifully rounded voice filled the church. Everyone fell silent, enthralled by the unexpected voice that now flowed through the church, giving it warmth and life. When they finished, the butler suggested "Silent Night." They ran through the butler's repertoire of sacred songs and added a few secular songs, but in honor of God.

"What a lovely day I had," Lotte said, as the two women walked home. Lotte held my hand and Mutti held Lisl's. "I can face anything now," Lotte said.

"Everybody is happy," I said, with an air of satisfaction.

As we approached the plant, Mutti said goodbye to the villagers. They replied, *"Ate logo, ate amanha"* (which means "see you tomorrow" in Portuguese) as they walked away, chattering and singing cheerfully.

"Everything is all right again," I said.

I had been looking forward to the priests' coming for months but later, as I listened to the priest talking with Mutti, I began to feel so tired that I hardly cared any more. I was exhausted. I slunk back to the house. I felt chilled and began to shake. I wrapped myself in a blanket and lay down.

Mutti came looking for me. She found me in bed, sound asleep. She touched my forehead and found it hot. She hurried out, looking for Papa. But the first person she met was one of the priests.

"Poor Hansi," she said. "He'd been so looking forward to your coming and now he has a fever and is asleep at home. I'm just looking for his father."

"Let me look at him," the priest said. He felt my forehead, looked at me, and said, "I'm not a doctor, but it looks like a typical case of malaria. I have some quinine pills. Let me give you two. They should help him recover."

Malaria, a common disease in Brazil at that time, can be fatal if untreated but the standard treatment, quinine, is very effective. Quinine was available in more developed areas but unlikely to be stocked in backcountry villages, so traveling priests carried their own supply.

Papa arrived just as the priest was about to leave and he concurred with the diagnosis. The quinine pills worked well for me and I began to recover from the malaria.

A few days later, I seemed well enough that Papa decided to go to the nearby town of São Francisco with Paolo to begin work on establishing a location where local farmers could drop off their cassava root. That was a new idea; it would save the farmers from having to bring their crops all the way to the plant or waiting for one of the plant trucks to pick them up. Papa expected to spend two or three days there.

The day after he left, Lisl was shivering in bed. It was probably malaria but Mutti could not be sure and did not have quinine if it were. She needed Papa by her side to use his professional skills. She rushed out, looking for the baron, who was usually lying under a vehicle and tinkering with it. She saw him across the way, rushed over and asked him to send a truck to get Papa. "Sorry, I can't do that," the baron replied. "We need the trucks for work."

Mutti persisted, but the baron still refused. Then someone spoke up, saying, "I will be happy to do whatever the doctor and his family need. I'll get the doctor." It was Tiburcio speaking. The baron said no more. He knew that Tiburcio was respected by all the workers. It was not a fight he wanted.

Papa took only minutes to determine that Lisl had malaria — and a bad case, likely due to her small size. He gave her some quinine and Mutti put damp cloths on her forehead. There was little to do but wait it out. I was recovering steadily but still in bed as well.

The day after Lisl came down with malaria, Marie, the baroness' daughter, stopped by to ask Mutti to cook dinner. Apologizing,

Mutti said she had to stay with her sick children.

Marie replied, "I had no idea your children were ill. I guess little children catch lots of things. So what you are saying is that you won't come to cook for us."

"I am sorry to be unable to do that while the children are ill," Mutti replied.

Marie said over her shoulder as she left, "I'll tell my mother."

We both recovered fine but a relapse of malaria may have been the cause when my sister was bedridden for some time when we were teenagers. I never suffered a recurrence but my malaria left its mark. Whenever I donate blood I have to say that I had malaria, resulting in a procedure that strips the platelets from the blood for use; the rest is discarded.

Recovery from malaria is best supported with good nutrition. Unfortunately our diets were limited. We rarely ate meat in Barra. No butcher shops existed in the town and itinerant butchers who traveled from town to town bringing a cow to slaughter had seen no reason to come to Barra. But once the mill started up and word spread that people began to have some money, a butcher arrived with a cow. I heard about it and followed some of the women who were going to buy meat from the butcher.

Partway out of town, a post stood planted in the ground. The butcher tied the cow to the post and then hit it on the forehead with a big wooden mallet, knocking it out. The butcher then had the women place basins under the cow's neck to catch the blood when he cut its neck. The blood was considered valuable. When the bleeding stopped, the butchering would begin.

I went home to tell Mutti about it. "Show me quickly," Mutti said. "I'd like to get some meat if I can." As Mutti and I arrived at the site, a cluster of women pressed around the butcher, who was cutting meat off the carcass. He was selling the meat by the size of the piece. Mutti later said, "That's the first time I ever bought meat by the hand width." As we reached the group, Marianna and Xixi turned to Mutti and said, "Dona Theresa, we bought you a nice piece of meat."

When we got home, Mutti was excited about cooking something different than our usual diet of beans, fish or shrimp. She was going to make the most of this rare delicacy. She was going to sauté the meat and use the pan juices to make gravy for the rice. That sounded wonderful to me.

Dr. Myers Arrives

One day in June after school, I decided to watch the ship dock. A small crowd had gathered but it wasn't until the baron showed up that we realized someone important was on board. With a big smile and an outstretched hand, the baron greeted a new arrival, a heavy-set, pale man with thinning blond hair. He wore a light, wrinkled seersucker suit and carried himself with an air of importance. He appeared to expect people to step aside and make room for him as he moved through the crowd.

At the plant, the baron spotted Papa and introduced him to the man, Dr. Myers, saying he had met him in São Paolo. "He has a lot of experience and will be a big help to us here."

The baron added, "Myers will be in charge of finding ways to improve our processes and operations. He will handle the technical part of our operations. I am sure that you fellows will get along well." He gave my father a big smile and a pat on the back.

Papa, on hearing the scope of Myers' responsibilities, was taken aback. He had imagined that he would remain in general charge. But he had been a soldier and he knew about orders. He nodded assent to the baron.

Just then Tiburcio walked by with his arm in a sling. Seeing him, Papa shouted, "Senhor, how is your arm?'

As Tiburcio yelled back, "Just fine; thank you."

Myers chuckled and then laughed. "What's so funny?" the baron asked.

"Calling a black man 'Senhor,' that's really rich," Myers answered.

Papa was upset. "Tiburcio is the foreman and the most respected man in the plant," he said with an edge in his voice. Myers still chuckled.

That evening, Mutti sensed that Papa was not in his usual good mood. He explained about Myers, adding, "My first contact with Myers gives me some concern. I had the sense that he was one of those Germans with a superior attitude and had little respect for the local people. That could be troublesome."

Papa was right to be concerned about Myers, as events would prove.

As time went on, I realized there was something about Myers that I did not like: His behavior changed when the baron was traveling. If the baron was at dinner, Myers spent most of his time talking to him, looking very serious. When the baron was traveling, Myers became very attentive to the baroness; he complimented her on her dress or some other article of clothing and gave her ingratiating smiles. The baroness blushed but seemed to like the attention. If Marie was at dinner, Myers was also very gallant to her. With the others at the table, Myers was different. He was courteous but distant with Kolszinski and was abrupt with Mutti, Papa and Franzen. They seemed of little interest to him. Lisl and I were not worthy of notice, except as annoyances. Over time, it seemed to me that the baroness looked forward to Myers' attention and his compliments. She accepted that when the baron was present, Myers would focus mainly on him.

Myers' careful and sustained effort to build a relationship with the baron and the baroness were behind an unwelcome development.

Mutti, Lotte, Lisl and I were walking back to the house when the baroness pulled up next to us in her car. "Mrs. Weiser," she called out, "you and your family will have to move out of our house."

Mutti answered, "Yes, I know we are to move when our house is ready."

"No," the baroness said, "you have to move now. Dr. Myers needs additional space for his work and plans to use the rooms you are occupying. Since your house is not ready yet, you can move into the laboratory building on the plant site."

Lotte interrupted, "But that's dangerous."

The baroness replied with a steely gaze, "No more dangerous than it is for Dr. Weiser right now."

Mutti cut in, "Yes, Baroness, we'll pack up tonight and move tomorrow."

The baroness answered, "Very good," and drove off.

Lotte was upset. "That woman!" she cried. "What nerve! Just asks you to pick up and move your family at the drop of a hat, and where does she put you? Right in the middle of the operations. We're just pawns to her."

"It's okay," Mutti said. "It should be only a short while before our house is finished and we can manage until then."

You would have thought that Myers, a single man by himself, could have worked in the laboratory building rather than in the house. After all, it was an industrial building and not at all meant to be lived in, especially by a family with children. But Myers asked for our rooms and the baron agreed. It bothered me that we had to leave the baron's house where those in charge lived. I'm sure my parents recognized that our departure also meant that Myers would have the baron and his family all to himself, with no one to mitigate his influence.

The next day, we moved to the one-story laboratory building, which stood on the side of the site facing the mill and adjacent to the machine shop. It was the seventh place we had lived in since we left Vienna.

I am not sure that Lotte was right about the site being dangerous but we were in the middle of the noisy action. As you stepped out the door, the mill was directly in front of you, the machine shop on your left almost attached to the same building. And of course trucks came and went, some bringing tapioca roots and others taking bags of flour away. The baron's house was to the right, several hundred yards away.

The move to the laboratory building posed some challenges, especially for Mutti. The narrow building had three rooms. You entered in the middle room, with the other rooms extending on either side. The room on the left remained as a combination work and storage room. The entry room served as our kitchen, dining and living room. The other room became our bedroom, where Papa and Mutti shared one larger bed and Lisl and I shared a smaller bed. We coped with the small space but cooking was a challenge for Mutti. I guess we had been spoiled at the baron's house, which had a good-sized kitchen as well as a cook and other people to help.

The main challenge for Mutti was the stove. It was the first time she had used a wood-burning stove. Mutti would arrange larger pieces of wood in the firebox and put some kindling on top. Then she would carefully put some kerosene as starter fluid and throw in a match. She had to make sure that she did not put in too much kerosene; otherwise, she'd have to jump back to avoid being burned by the blowback.

A second problem was that the stove's cooking area was only big enough for one pot. As a result, Mutti often had to beg for space on someone else's stove. That made cooking a production: First Mutti would have to ask different women for space on their stoves; then bring pots to the stoves; and later retrieve them with the cooked food.

I suppose Mutti and Papa may have missed the adult conversation at the baron's house, but for Lisl and me, eating with Mutti and Papa and talking with them at meals was better than sitting at the baron's table, where we were expected to be quiet.

The laboratory building was intended to be utilitarian. It had no windows on the back wall; the single windows in each room on the plant side provided light but were too high for me to look out. I could only look out through the door when it was open. One of the villagers, probably Xixi, planted flowers for us on either side of the front door to brighten the place up. I still worked in my garden by Lotte's house but also enjoyed trimming the flowers by the laboratory. Maybe the flowers were out of place in an industrial zone but I think the men didn't mind the color and happiness of the flowers against the white wall of the building.

What I remember best about our new home was the space behind it. The back of the building was a plain white stucco wall. A high fence separated it from a storage yard next door. The narrow space between wall and fence had little moving air and attracted mosquitoes. They were easy to spot as they rested on the white stucco and I took great pleasure in killing as many as I could.

Mosquitoes were a big problem. While malaria was the big risk, the more common problem arose from scratching bites. The broken skin brought on infections at a time before antibiotics existed. Mutti often walked around with cheesecloth bandages on her lower legs, covering open sores, and I still carry scars on my legs from the bites that got seriously infected.

From the lab building, it was very common to see the baron working on his car. Sometimes as I'd walk by, he'd yell out from underneath, "Hansi, go into the shop and ask them to give you a monkey wrench for me," or it might be pliers or some other tool. One day, as he was standing by the open hood of the car, he told me to look at the pistons. "They run up and down and drive the crankshaft that makes the wheels turn." He saw my quizzical look and laughed. "Don't worry, you'll figure it out soon enough. Off you go."

He was that way. He'd often ask me to fetch something for him or tell me what he was doing. He was nice to me but I heard that with others he could be a big scary bear of a man. People said that if things went wrong, it was best to stay away from him because he could get very angry and anybody near him would feel the brunt of it.

Not long after we moved into the lab building, the baron was about to leave for another trip to Rio. Before he left, he called in Papa, Myers, Paolo and Enrique. He said, "I'm leaving Arthur in charge of the facility. I expect you all to cooperate with him."

Papa responded, "Thank you, Baron. But it may be too much. I think you should put Dr. Myers in charge of something as well."

The baron looked a bit pained but rallied and said, "Okay, Myers, you be in charge of the engine facilities."

Myers said, "Fine."

Paolo looked uneasy, since in fact he had done all the work on the engine room so far. But he decided to swallow his pride and accept the situation.

A few days later, Papa heard the engine making an erratic noise. He found Myers and asked him to come and listen to the engine. Myers came, stopped, cocked his head and looked as if he were listening. After a bit, he said, "I don't hear anything. I am sure that if there is some noise, I'll hear it in due course. Right now, I want to search out potential living quarters for my family. Good-bye." And without waiting for an answer, he left.

Papa was concerned about Myers' puzzling behavior. Meanwhile, I was feeling sad. I was alone in our rooms in the laboratory, crying. I was overcome by homesickness for Rio. I missed Father Alphonso and Dona Teresinha, who were really good friends. And I missed the beach, the people, the trolleys, the shops. Mutti surprised me when she came in. I thought I'd just cry by myself.

"What's the matter, Hansi?" she asked as she put her arms around me.

"I miss Father Alphonso and Dona Teresinha," I wailed. "The teacher here is not nearly as nice as Dona Teresinha."

"But she is a very nice woman," Mutti said.

"They are all nice in Barra," I replied. "They are all friendly and helpful but it's just not the same as with Father Alphonso. And then there are no priests here all the time. There's just the regular people in the church. There has been no priest to say Mass since the visiting priests left. It's just not the same."

"Well," Mutti said, "I have an idea. Why don't you write Father Alphonso and ask him to send us some priests." So I wrote the letter and asked Franzen to mail it. I felt much better, believing my request to be in good hands.

I was never able to determine if Father Alphonso sent them, but sure enough the priests who visited us earlier came back again. Right after the first Mass, one of the priests approached Mutti and signaled that they should step away from the others leaving the church. "Mrs. Weiser, I have some bad news for you," he said.

"What is it?" she asked.

"Just before we left Rio, a woman who lives at your old boarding house told me the police came around asking about your husband. Apparently they think he is a spy," the priest said.

My mother told him that the spy claim was a misunderstanding.

He replied, "It may be a misunderstanding, but it might be best if you go back to Rio and lose yourselves in the crowd or maybe move further into the country. Here you are very visible."

The conversation left Mutti feeling worried that the old spy scare was back again and the family could face renewed trouble. She was disturbed that Brazil's concern about being drawn into the war in Europe could now be threatening our family, even far out in the backcountry. She told Papa about the alarming message from the priest and about how much it upset her.

Another cause for concern arose when Mutti went to the baron's house to return a knife she had borrowed. When she was in the kitchen, she overheard some voices coming from the next room. She moved a bit closer. It was Myers, saying, "Baron, Dr. Weiser is not the man to run the plant. That is not his profession and he is much too sympathetic to the workers. You can afford experts. Let Weiser do what he does best and let someone with real experience run the operation."

That evening Mutti told Papa what she had heard. Papa said, "I can't quite figure out what Myers is up to. Is he pushing me out so he can run the plant? Or is he pushing me out just to push me out? In either event, the plant is running well and the men are working diligently. I think the baron sees that and is not going to make a change just because Myers suggests it."

Mutti was not happy to leave it there. After dinner, she told Papa that she wanted to talk to Lotte and went to the bachelors' house. Once there, Mutti told Lotte, Franzen, Paolo and Enrique what she had overheard.

Paolo said, "I have my own thoughts about Myers. He told us that he earned his doctorate at Gaerung Institute. Well, that institute doesn't give doctoral degrees."

Franzen added, "He told us that he was 36 years old and had lived in Brazil since 1924. Taking into account his years of study, the numbers don't add up."

They all told Mutti that they would watch Myers and be on the alert for any unusual actions.

A New House and an Old Curse

One day the baroness came to find Mutti to show her the house we would be moving into. Lisl and I tagged along. As we walked by the plant, the baroness took the opportunity to make a comment about Papa. "Dr. Weiser doesn't look too well," she said. "Dr. Myers seems to stand the climate better. Of course, he's younger."

Mutti explained about our limited diet. "We don't get canned food from Campos or Rio. There's no butcher shop in town, and if there were he'd be of little use because the cattle are so scrawny that the meat is like leather. People don't keep geese or ducks because they might escape to the river. Most of the fishermen are now working at the plant. So we live mostly on shrimp caught by the boys. We have shrimp almost every day — boiled, fried, breaded, rolled in cheese, with banana blossoms. I hate them."

"Why don't you let your husband eat with us and you just manage with the children?" the baroness asked.

Mutti was quiet. Papa was working himself to exhaustion for the baron. Now they wanted to take away from him the few minutes he had at the end of the day for rest and family to refresh himself?

They kept walking on, past the machine shop, where the baroness said, "Now you can see the house."

The baroness was pointing at a small white house some distance away, with a thatched roof, new and still light-colored. It stood on a small rise. Wildflowers and plants shouldered each other in the uncultivated grounds and there was a banana tree off to one side. Beyond, in the near distance, a stand of old, large trees grew into the sky. Mutti turned to Lisl and me and said, "It looks beautiful, doesn't it?"

I thought it was wonderful. Our own house. Much bigger than the laboratory rooms — but mainly our own house, and with room for a garden, and on a rise so you could see down the street and look all around. I hoped we could move soon.

Mutti and the baroness went inside. I started to walk around. Beside the house there was a large open pasture where a horse was grazing. Beyond the pasture, open, uncultivated land extended out, spotted with just shrubs, bushes and clumps of grass. In the distance, the mountains took shape.

A few minutes later, Mutti came out with a worried look but an air of determination. "Wait here," she ordered. "I have to get some medicine. There's a sick woman lying in there on the floor. Some children are with her, some of whom also look sick."

Soon, Mutti was back with some quinine pills. When she came out, she said she was going to get some water at the baron's house for the woman and her children. As we approached the laboratory, Mutti saw Papa. She said, "I've got good news for you. You'll be eating with the baron and baroness from now on."

"You too?" Papa asked.

"Of course not, you silly. Who'd be with the children?"

"I'm not going," Papa replied.

Mutti waved goodbye. She thought, "Of course, he'll eat with the baron. He likes my company but he also likes good food."

Going back to the new house with the water, Mutti met the baroness, who asked, "When are you going to move?"

"When the woman is well enough to leave the house," Mutti said. "And when the floors are finished and the windows and doors are set and I've had a chance to clean the place."

"My God," the Baroness replied, "what a fuss we make over these Negroes. They're used to creeping in a dirty hole and finishing their illnesses there."

Mutti thought, Never mind what she says, think of what she does. The baroness did stay to watch the sick woman until she was asleep.

Finally, the day came: Our house was finished and we moved in. It was the first house we had to ourselves since leaving Vienna some eighteen months earlier, and it was a wonderful change from the laboratory building. Papa and Mutti had their own room, as did Lisl and I. And Lisl and I had separate beds. There was a separate kitchen and a nice living and dining room.

Mutti remained worried about mosquitoes. Both Lisl and I slept under white, see-through mosquito nets that hung from the ceiling and draped over the posts at the four ends of our beds to try to stave off any bites or new exposure to malaria.

There was some open space around the house and Mutti set aside a piece for me to have a garden. I gave Lotte my old garden

Papa, Mutti and Lisl together in Barra.

and concentrated on this new one. Xixi helped me again with some plants and I replanted some flowers from my old garden. Pretty quickly it looked very nice.

Now that we had our own house, Mutti thought it appropriate for us to have a maid. Zenida was a young girl who had large teeth and a smile so wide that Lisl said it made her think of a nutcracker.

One day, Mutti saw Zenida with a lump under her dress and told her to take it out. Soon one of Lisl's dresses was back on a hook. Zenida laughed and said, "When someone has so much and the other nothing, don't you think they should share?"

We may have had our own house, but Mutti was still aware of what was going on at the baron's house. Dona Maria, the villager who had cooked for the baroness, had been dismissed when the cook Laura arrived. A stout, blond woman with rosy cheeks who wore dirndl dresses, Laura had arrived not long after Myers, introducing herself as "the cook for the baron and baroness," intoned in way that conveyed her understanding of the importance of the position.

Dona Maria was not happy about the abrupt change and as revenge, placed a voodoo curse on the house by leaving three dead chickens on Laura's doorstep. Laura, unaware of the local meaning of three dead chickens on your doorstep, thought they were a gift, looked at them, found them fine and cleaned and cooked them.

Two young village girls, Hermina and Belinda, who worked as maids at the baroness' house, were horrified by Laura's action and fled. Mutti and I were walking back to the house when we met them. Mutti asked why they were hurrying.

The girls told us the story of the voodoo curse. "There are evil spirits in the house," they said. "We are not comfortable there."

Mutti looked squarely at the girls and said, "Please remember what the priests taught you. If you ever feel an evil spirit, make the sign of the cross, say a quick prayer and the evil spirit will flee. You do not have to be afraid."

The two girls thought about that but still seemed uneasy. Belinda said, "They call us little Negro girls and do not respect us."

Mutti replied, "You certainly deserve respect. But think for a moment. You both are wearing beautiful blouses and very nice skirts and you look well because you are eating well. And it is because the baron is paying you for your work. And look at Antonio over there. He has a new shirt. And it's all because the baron built his mill here and is paying you all salaries. People now have money and butchers are coming, bringing cows for meat, and Vargas is regularly driving his truck to Campos to bring supplies. The whole village is better off. Don't quit your jobs at the baron's house. Go and earn the money to buy the things you need and want."

Hermina was persuaded and pressed Belinda to go back. They waved to us as they walked back to the baron's house.

Later that day, a butcher arrived again. Mutti bought some fresh meat for us but also bought a piece for the baron's house. When Mutti handed it to Laura, the cook said, "You really do run this village, don't you? This morning you had the two girls come back here and now you find fresh meat. It's all a mystery to me."

Mutti answered, "It's really not hard. I just love them all dearly."

What Is Myers Up To?

Papa came in. He looked sick. His jaw was red, swollen and looked ugly; a scratch must have gotten infected. He did not even see me as he headed straight for the medicine box. The box was empty. He sat down fatigued. There was a knock at the door.

It was Paolo, waving a small card in his hand. "It's a work permit," he said.

"How did you get it?" Papa asked. "They are very difficult to get."

"Myers helped me. He sent me to a clerk in Niterói, near Rio. I mentioned Myers' name and I got the permit," Paolo said.

"Sounds too easy," Papa said.

"Well, you know, I have this scar on my face and Myers thinks it's a dueling scar, the kind that German upper-class men get in fencing duels. So he thinks I am a good Aryan and he trusts me. In fact he just asked me to strike," Paolo said.

"What are you talking about?" Papa asked, incredulously.

"He wants to get me away from here. He already dismissed Alfredinho and if I'm gone, there will be no engineers on site. Machines might malfunction and there'd be no one here to fix them."

"Why would he want that?" Papa asked.

"I am not sure but I do know that Myers is in a 'higher' service. He has German contacts," Paolo said, implying that Myers might be working for the German war effort.

Just then, the baron stepped in the door. Papa told him that

Myers had asked Paolo to strike.

The baron laughed. "What would be the purpose of that? Let me tell you what really concerns me. The government seems to be reducing the amount of tapioca that flour manufacturers have to include in their flour. If we can't sell what we produce, we'll be out of business."

"Do you think there might be people in the government trying to take advantage of their ability to manipulate the quota?" Papa asked.

"God, I hadn't thought of that. If it's people in the government, they could destroy us. We're probably just foreigners to them," the baron moaned.

"On the other hand," Papa said, "if it's someone trying to take advantage of the quota, they could be just moving into the milling business. They might have other businesses running right now. Perhaps you can find ways to engage them in their current business as suppliers or customers and provide them a good reason for avoiding all the problems of starting up something new."

"That is good thinking," said the baron. Looking at Papa and Paolo, he added, "I knew that if we worked together, we'd figure it out. We're partners in all this. Good work." And he walked back to the house with a jaunty step.

"Kolszinski is a good man," Papa told Mutti one evening. "Matthias somehow got drunk and Kolszinski arranged an almost formal hearing about the situation with Matthias. It turns out that Matthias had gotten into Myers' room and found some liquor and drank it all. Myers did not want to admit he had any liquor with him so he denied it." Papa started to laugh and continued, "So Kolszinski decided that since no one reported any liquor missing, Matthias couldn't have been drunk."

"I wonder what Matthias was doing in Myers' room?" Mutti asked.

"I think he was spying on Myers, trying to find out something about Myers' other activities," Papa said. He explained that Matthias had discovered that Myers was writing for a newspaper in São Paulo. Kolszinski had said, "I've learned that Myers is actually working for an organization with ties to Germany. He's writing articles for newspapers trying to persuade Brazil to join the war effort on the side of Germany."

"Oh my goodness," said Mutti. "We don't need a Nazi here. That could be trouble."

"I don't really think so," Papa said. "First, I don't think the Brazilians would ally with Germany, but even if they did, the war is in Europe. Brazil might send help, but I don't think it would change everyday life in Brazil itself. And anyway, we are way out here in the country, a long way from the big city where political activity takes place. We have enough problems of our own. We can't worry about those possibilities."

That was the last I heard about that until the very end. But there was more to Paolo's story.

One day I could hear a commotion out in the plant yard and went to look. Paolo, very angry, was being held by two policemen. Myers stood nearby with a black eye. A large number of workers from the mill were standing in a group, leaning toward the policemen.

Papa asked one of the policemen, "What's going on?" The policeman responded that they had been ordered to pick Paolo up and take him to Campos because he had an illegal work permit.

The workers were angry and wanted to intervene, but Paolo said, "Thanks, my friends. Let's let these men do their job. I'm sure it will all work out in the end."

Hearing the shouting, the baroness came out of her house. The first person she saw was Myers, with his black eye. "Dear Dr. Myers, what happened to you?" she asked.

Myers said that Paolo had punched him because he thought Myers had something to do with the arrest. "It was a misunderstanding."

"You poor man. And that brute. You're too generous," cooed the baroness, as she led Myers back into the house, "Come in and let's see if there is something for your eye."

Papa looked sadly at the disappearing figure of Paolo and remembered that it was Myers who had sent Paolo to get what now was seen as an illegal work permit.

A few days after Paolo's arrest, I was with Papa in the laboratory building. He was testing some liquid from the mill, when we heard an explosion. Papa jumped up, told me, "Wait here," and rushed out. I stood by the door and looked. There was a cloud of smoke over the mill and flames appeared to be flickering in the building. Men were rushing out of the mill and running away from the building.

Papa rushed into the building. It seemed as if he was in there a long time. The men who had fled the building were now milling around by the machine shop, presumably a safe distance away. We all waited. The flames slowly died down and then finally Papa and Tiburcio came out. They looked like black twins; both their faces and their clothes were black with soot and ashes.

Papa told Mutti that the engine in the mill had overheated and caused the oil in the machine to catch fire. The explosion must have been from a can of kerosene nearby. Papa and Tiburcio had used dirt to put the fire out, choking it of air, because water might have just spread the burning oil around the mill.

Kolszinski came by later to thank Papa. He went on, "What really upsets me is that after the explosion, Myers said it was all part of a plan. He told the baroness that the machine was not the right one and needed to be replaced. Since it was still under warranty Myers decided to allow it to destroy itself." According to Kolszinski, the baroness thought Myers very clever for his ploy.

Perhaps still celebrating his success, Myers decided to go Rio to visit his family and to have a doctor there double-check an infection in his leg that Papa had already looked at. At the same time, Laura, the cook, was entitled to some time off and also decided to go to Rio. They were to be gone almost two weeks.

The baron liked company and the baroness liked a cook in the kitchen. As a result, while the others were away, our family was invited once again to join them at dinner — and to prepare dinner. The meals were pleasant and enjoyable. The baron and baroness were gracious and the conversation friendly and light. Even Lisl and I, though mostly silent and observing, could see that Papa and Mutti were enjoying themselves. I did not turn on the radio for the national anthem.

When Myers and Laura returned, the gossip was that Laura had spent all her time and money at the casino and that Myers had gotten the same advice from the doctors in Rio that Papa had given him.

It wasn't long before Myers' hand was visible again. A big feast day was coming. October 4 would mark the feast of St. Francis, the saint to whom the village was dedicated. Brazilians love to celebrate and this day was traditionally an occasion for a big party and picnic. The villagers would congregate at the church and then slowly walk for two hours to a small chapel that stood in a meadow near the top of a hill. The meadow was the place for the picnic. Villagers were happily getting the food ready and preparing their outfits for the day.

At the baron's house, voices were being raised. Myers argued that they should not shut the factory down for the feast day and the baron agreed.

Papa responded, "No, no. You must understand. This happens once a year. It is a very important day for the workers. The factory normally runs seven days a week. This is a very rare exception. Keeping the workers from their annual pilgrimage will kill morale and we'll pay for it for a long time."

Myers spoke up: "Don't worry, Baron. Weiser doesn't have the stomach for this. I'll take care of it."

The next morning the sun rose on a beautiful day. Villagers were busy getting ready, putting on their festive clothes and preparing the picnic food. There was chatting, giggling and happy laughter.

Suddenly there was a wrenching scream and a wail from the church. Villagers ran to the sound. They found a table set with ritual foods associated with a dreaded voodoo curse. The happy spirits of the day fizzled like air from a pricked balloon. The pilgrimage and the picnic were abandoned.

There was nothing left to do but shuffle grudgingly to work.

The evening of the ruined feast, Tiburcio and Vargas knocked on our door.

Tiburcio said, "We have been talking in the village. We have a pretty good idea who set up that table of the dead. We think the same man is making trouble for you at the baron's house. We decided to put our money together and hire you ourselves as our doctor. We'll try to match what the baron is paying you."

Papa had to pause and catch his breath. He knew what a sacrifice it was for the villagers to hire him as a doctor. He was genuinely moved but he said he could not break his contract with the baron.

The next morning Kolszinski told Papa, "I heard about that offer last night. Forget about it. You are too valuable and we won't let you out of your contract."

"Nothing stays quiet for long in a village, does it?" said Papa. "Don't worry, I told them I mean to keep my commitment."

Eventually Paolo returned from Campos. People crowded around, welcoming him back and pouring questions at him. Paolo was deeply moved. He explained that the judge had decided it was just a misunderstanding and freed him.

Mutti sent me to tell Papa of Paolo's arrival. We came to the group around Paolo and Papa shook his hand and gave him a light abraço. Papa and I walked with him to the bachelors' quarters.

"Do you think that Kolszinski or the baron or even Myers had something to do with your release?" Papa asked.

"I don't know, but it would have been nice if Myers had admitted that he set me up." Paolo said.

Papa said, "I think you ought to apologize to him."

"Are you kidding?" Paolo asked.

"You are going to be working for him. He's your boss," Papa went on. "It's best to clear the air and get this behind you. I know you have to swallow some pride to do it but I think it will make your working relationship easier."

The timing was excellent because as we approached the baron's house, Myers and the baroness were coming out. They did not seem surprised to see Paolo. Somebody must have gotten the news to them.

"Good to see you, Paolo," Myers boomed.

Paolo bristled but said in a steady voice, "Thank you, Dr. Myers. I'd like to apologize for losing my temper when the police came to pick me up. I am sorry."

"No need to apologize. It was a misunderstanding. Glad to have you back," Myers said, in an overly jovial tone.

The baroness glowed at Myers' magnanimity.

Christmas 1940

Christmas Day arrived. Two Christmases before we were in Hungary and it had just snowed. Here in Brazil, Mutti, Papa, Lotte, Franzen, Paolo and Enrique were going to the beach. I went along but Lisl wanted to stay with three of the teenage village girls. The girls could not get enough of Lisl — this beautiful child with light golden curls who behaved as if she were the equal of the older girls, although she was half their age.

We got to the beach by boat down the river from Barra. Like the beach in Rio, this one had beautiful white sand and crashing waves. But unlike Rio, the beach here seemed to run endlessly to the horizon, a strip of white with the blue ocean on one side and green mountains on the other. And it seemed like your private beach because the only people in sight were the handful of Europeans from Barra.

Mutti said that she always enjoyed the beach, allowing the cool waves to wash over her, walking down the beach toward the mouth of the river, looking for beautiful shells and then lying back on a bed of lichen and enjoying the sun. Today there was a subdued feeling to the group, as people spoke of Christmas back in Europe.

Mutti said, "We always had baked carp. It was a tradition. Arthur hates fat fish but he ate it, because it was the tradition."

Paolo added, "We always had ham at Christmas."

Lotte spoke up, "Those happy memories. Will we ever see those days again?"

"Soon the Americans will join in the war and there will be bombs all over Germany," Enrique responded. "Then we'll have our revenge."

"I don't mind their smashing all the munitions factories and whatever they need to destroy to bring the war to an end," Lotte said. "I just hope they don't bomb our lime tree. Franzen, you remember our lime tree, don't you?"

"They won't bomb our lime tree," Franzen said soothingly.

"And the church where I used to sit with my father and the meadows with the blackberry bushes around and the marigolds," Lotte continued.

"Oh, skip it," Paolo said and got up, ran to the water and jumped in.

I went in the water a few times to cool off. Then I dried off because I wanted to join Getúlio, a villager who owned a rowboat and brought us to the beach. I enjoyed riding in the boat and sometimes Getúlio allowed me to row.

Around midday, there was flurry of excitement and a scare. Papa was waving from the beach like he wanted the boat in a big hurry. When we got to the beach, Papa asked me to get out and wait while he and Paolo put Mutti in the boat. She was very pale, with almost a bluish cast, and seemed to be asleep.

Papa said, "Don't worry, Hansi. Mutti will be fine. She's had too much sun and needs some time in the shade and some rest. You wait here with the boys and Getúlio will bring you back as fast as he can." Lotte went with Papa and Mutti in the boat.

When I got back to the village, I found Lisl and brought her home. By then Mutti was lying quietly in bed sleeping and Papa told us that she would be fine. Still Lisl and I worried. We had never seen Mutti sick.

Mutti finally woke up a few hours later. We had all been waiting anxiously. When she woke, Lisl and I ran to her bed to share an important discovery. "It's a miracle, a miracle," Lisl exclaimed. "We found holly in the woods. It was there just for us; it wasn't there before."

I added, "I saw it on a tree where it didn't belong, but we collected it just in time for Christmas."

With Papa's help, Lisl and I had put some garlands on the top of the mirror and I explained to Mutti, "We hung garlands on the mirror so you can see them twice." We had also found a small tree with blossoms on it, brought it home and trimmed it. Next to the tree Papa placed a small wooden crèche he and Mutti had brought from Vienna. It was small and the paint had flaked, but it was still beautiful.

There was a knock on the door and Lotte entered with Franzen, Enrique, Paolo and Fritz. "Merry Christmas," they shouted.

Lotte gave me a small package and said, "This is my first Christmas present from Franzen, but I will let you use it."

It was a beautiful small radio and the timing was perfect. I turned on the radio and the national anthem was playing. I had it on loud but the adults didn't mind. They shouted over it. Eventually they joined in singing the anthem. When the anthem was finished, they turned off the radio and we sang Christmas carols.

Everybody enjoyed Christmas. It was especially wonderful because we finally had a house of our own.

A Terrible Accident

The driver for Truck No. 4, Joaquim, was a new hire. He was not a regular driver but the baron had hired him because he knew the local roads.

One day in January 1941, four trucks headed to Campos loaded with sacks of tapioca flour to be loaded on railcars. Truck 4 was unloaded first so Joaquim could run errands for Laura and the baroness while the others worked on unloading the other trucks. The list was fairly long; there were at least four stops. As it turned out, there were as many bars as there were shops and Joaquim must have stopped in each of them. When it was time to return to Barra, the empty trucks met at the central square. There they picked up a crowd of passengers who had seized the rare opportunity for a ride into Campos and back home. A plant worker named Demetrios, seven students and four women climbed into the open back of Truck 4.

The trucks began as a convoy, one after the other, with Truck 4 in the rear, but Joaquim was having some trouble keeping up with the others. They were within a half hour of home when they came to a sharp turn. Joaquim continued to drive straight; then, realizing his error, he turned the steering wheel sharply to the left to make the sharp turn. But the truck, with its mass and weight, had its own momentum. The truck toppled over and ended on its side, wheels spinning, on the bank below the road.

All the passengers, who had been standing or sitting in the back of the truck, were thrown onto the hard earth. There was momentary silence, then screams pierced the air as the wounded yowled in pain and others screamed in panic and confusion, some suffering broken arms or legs or lacerations. Demetrios landed on his head. His neck broke and he died instantly.

Fortunately, it was only minutes before Truck 2 retraced the route to see where Truck 4 was. What the driver of Truck 2 found was much worse than the others had feared. He quickly drove to Barra to get Papa. As soon as Papa understood the magnitude of the accident, he swung into action. He grabbed Enrique, who had some first aid training, and Fritz, gathered whatever medical supplies he had and got on the truck, telling the driver, "Go as fast as you can without killing us."

On the way, Papa explained to Enrique the principle of triage: those who need immediate help, those who can wait an hour or two, and finally those who can wait longer. At the scene, he set to work, stopping bleeding and helping those who were having trouble breathing. Fritz organized a group of workers to load the wounded into the trucks and then to carefully unload them at the plant, where Tiburcio and others had cleared the bays in the garage and set up a large table to be Papa's operating room. Enrique was assisting.

The most challenging were two victims suffering with possible internal injuries or internal bleeding. Papa could only keep them under observation and possibly send them to the hospital in Campos. Fortunately there were no injuries so urgent that Papa would have had to operate immediately to save lives. Even though the surgeon was excellent, the conditions were too primitive to ensure a good outcome.

The accident happened in the late afternoon. By the time the victims had been sorted and treated at the scene, it was already

evening. Papa was not able to start his work in his makeshift operating room until close to midnight. He, Enrique and Fritz worked
through the night. Tiburcio, Vargas and others took turns napping
and then helping to keep the kerosene lamps burning and moving
patients to the table and, when finished, back to their mats.

In the morning, the baroness came. "I heard that the patients
are lying on the ground. Is that true?'

"Yes, Baroness," said Papa. "They are on mats. Mats are what
they use at home." The baroness seemed surprised to discover that
the people didn't have beds.

Papa told her the police might want to question the driver,
because he didn't have a license. The baroness looked concerned.
"Is my husband likely to have any trouble?" she asked.

Papa reassured her. "The baron hired the driver because he was
familiar with the roads. He was meant to be driving trucks with
bags of flour. The baron did not anticipate that the truck would be
carrying passengers. He certainly did not intend to put anyone at
risk." The baroness seemed relieved.

But then she had a different kind of shock. Fritz, who had his
back to her, was not wearing a shirt. His bare back was filled with
burn scars in the form of crucifixes. "Oh my goodness, what happened to you?" the baroness asked.

"What does it look like?" Fritz asked. "The Nazis left me with
these scars because I was a leader in the Catholic workers' movement and the Nazis disapproved."

"All refugees I have ever met were Jewish," the baroness said. "I
thought it was only Jews who had fled Europe."

"That's mostly true, but the Nazis did their utmost to crush
anyone who opposed them." Fritz said.

Return to Rio

The German war effort and the Nazis had Brazilian officials concerned about spy efforts in Brazil. Very early one morning, Tiburcio came to our house and woke up my parents. He showed them a Campos newspaper he had just read with a headline blaring "WANTED" and below it a picture and description of Papa. It said Papa was wanted as a spy.

Tiburcio said that Papa should leave right away and that Tiburcio, his wife and other villagers would look after Mutti, Lisl and me. Papa embraced Tiburcio and said, "I never had a brother."

Mutti, Papa and Tiburcio discussed what might happen if my father were apprehended. Brazil had a number of internment camps and they discussed where he might be sent. In the end, Papa decided to go to Rio and face the issue.

Papa was gone ten days, which seemed interminable to Mutti. She had a vivid imagination and undoubtedly reviewed in her mind any number of frightening scenarios. Perhaps the police would consider Papa an accessory, based on his recommending the two young men to Becker. Perhaps they would conclude he was an accessory based on his several meetings with Becker. She had some sleepless nights. So it was a great relief when she learned he was returning to Barra.

The accusations of spying were related to Becker, who was an attaché of the British Embassy and who had been collecting sensitive information. Eventually, the authorities accepted that Papa was not involved.

While Papa was gone, the baron told Mutti with real delight that the German government had released road equipment that he owned, which had been trapped in Europe. It would be arriving in Brazil soon. Mutti realized what that might mean — that a new road to Campos might now be built, making it easier to get medical help from Campos. My father would therefore be less valuable to the baron. And it seemed to Mutti that the baron was not unhappy about that. Mutti wondered whether Myers had helped persuade the German government to release the equipment. From the time that Myers arrived, there was the possibility that he might replace Papa. Had he hurried this along?

Then, when Papa returned, Fritz told him that there was a new problem.

Papa kept morphine to use in treating serious injuries. When he went to Rio, he had told Fritz where the medicines were kept, in case they were needed for an emergency. Fritz decided to take the medicines to his room for safekeeping. Having found out about it, Myers was now threatening to have Papa arrested for leaving a narcotic with an unqualified person. The baron was siding with Myers. They offered an alternative to prosecution — that Papa resign. Myers had closed his net.

Papa did not have to think too long before he accepted the inevitable and signed the resignation. At home, he and Mutti discussed what to do next. There was the offer of the people of Barra to hire Papa as their doctor. But Papa had come to believe that Myers must be a Nazi, or at least a Nazi sympathizer. Besides his obvious desire to run the plant alone might be the deep anti-Semitism of a true Nazi. Papa said, "I believe that Myers would see my continued presence here as both a provocation and a challenge and would work hard to push me out by threatening to report me for practicing without a license. We'd be at risk all the time."

Somehow I heard that we would have to leave. Looking for me to tell me the news of our departure, Mutti found me lying on the ground crying in my flower garden. In my frustration and anger I had yanked out all the flowers.

We went to say goodbye to our friends, Lotte, Franzen, Enrique, Paolo and Fritz, who all knew about Papa being fired. Lotte, her belly now distended with pregnancy, put on a brave face and made some jokes, but as I thought about it later, I realized how much of a blow Mutti's leaving must have been to her. Mutti had become a good friend, really an older sister for her. As Mutti said once, "We have a lot in common. And being a refugee opens your eyes in many ways. Being torn from your home makes you realize the importance of human connections and bonds. You rebuild your life with friendships. You become aware of the importance of being generous, of reaching out to others to help and support. And you learn to accept help and generosity when it is extended to you."

For the factory workers, Papa had proved to be a fair and considerate boss. In addition, they felt the unfortunate effect of Papa's leaving; he had not only ministered to them as a local doctor might have, but also brought the skills of a highly trained European doctor. They would all miss him. Many of the villagers stopped by our house to say good-bye and wish us well.

But forces stronger than the kind sentiments of the people of Barra were at work. Those forces were pushing us forward again, into yet another chapter of our flight from Nazi Austria. After more than a year in the Brazilian backcountry, we packed up ourselves and our disappointment and headed back to Rio.

We slipped easily into our former patterns in Rio. There was a vacancy in the boarding house we had lived in by Ipanema Beach. It helped to be back in a familiar place, though living in one room was an abrupt change from our two-bedroom house in Barra. Still, we had the benefits of electricity, showers, indoor toilets, and all the color and life of Rio. The beach was down the block. And my parents were happy to greet old friends again.

I returned to school at Guy de Fontgalland. Unhappily (for me), Dona Teresinha had married and left the school but to my delight, Father Alphonso was still there. He welcomed me back warmly.

Dr. Campos accepted Papa back into his medical practice. There were uneasy moments when Papa saw a patient without Dr. Campos being present — he could have been charged with practicing without a local license. Still, the arrangement allowed Papa to use his professional training and to earn some money. Mutti slowly refreshed her list of pupils for piano and English lessons. One big change was that Lisl now went to school — an all-girls school run by an order of nuns. We enjoyed walking to school together in the morning.

The challenge now was to start over, searching again for ways of practicing medicine legally in Brazil — or, a more difficult challenge, to get a visa to another country.

One day Papa came home looking dejected with the news that France had fallen. He said, "With Hitler now holding all of continental Europe, I am afraid that Germany will take England. If that happens, the Nazis will be ruling for a long time. If we ever thought of returning, we now have to forget that possibility."

However, this development in the war brought an unexpected new opening for our family. Hungary allied itself with the triumphant Germany. As war raged, the United States severed diplomatic relations with Hungary, effectively cutting off the possibility for residents of Hungary to apply for visas to come to the U.S. At the same time, the U.S. kept the door open for Hungarians applying under an immigration quota. Papa could apply for entry for our family to the United States. He signed up quickly at the American Embassy in Rio and received the list of documents needed to support an application. Collecting those documents became Papa and

Mutti's top priority.

One evening, as we took a walk on the beautiful promenade along Ipanema Beach, we ran into the baron. "Well, what a wonderful surprise. I am delighted to see you all," he said with enthusiasm. He was either genuinely pleased to see us or a great faker. In his case either was possible.

"I am here continuing the struggle to retain the plant's quota," the baron continued as if he had never fired my father and as if my father still worried about the plant's quota.

Papa changed the subject. "Have you heard that France has fallen?" he asked.

The baron seemed impatient, "There is always some news from Europe," he retorted testily. "Frankly, I can't think about that. All I want is to know that my financial people got the money I had in Europe out of there. I can really only focus on my business here. That gives me enough to worry about. Good-bye." With that abrupt ending, he turned away. We never saw Baron Ludwig Kummer again.

As we approached our boarding house, we had another surprise. Fritz was waiting outside. He had left the baron's employ and was looking for work in Rio. He told us that the villagers had voted to try to get Papa back as their doctor. Papa was warmed by this, but he knew it would never work out. Besides, he and Mutti were now focused on getting into the U.S.

The biggest hurdle was to get someone in the United States to sponsor us or to provide financial backing for us. Papa and Mutti got busy writing letters to friends and acquaintances in Brazil and in the U.S.

After some months of effort, the day finally came for Papa to meet the U.S. consul. Mutti went along but first she needed to stop by the German Embassy to see if any documentation was needed from the German government. Since Austria had been taken over by Germany, the German Embassy would be the source of those documents. Lisl and I were in school but Mutti told us the story of what happened next. It was exciting and played to her natural storytelling gift.

Mutti left the German Embassy very disturbed and rushed to the American Consulate. She entered to find an attractive young Brazilian secretary and through an open door she could hear voices. One was Papa's. Mutti asked the secretary to take her in but the woman refused, with a condescending attitude. Mutti listened to the voices from the consul's office. In a warm and jovial voice, the consul was praising Papa. "You are quite a man. I have a pile of letters of recommendation for you. And they are from a remarkable range of people. I have one from a well-connected Mr. Kolszinski, from some Catholic priests, from a count who runs a Catholic refugee resettlement service, from a Brazilian doctor, from Jewish refugees, and from villagers way up in the backcountry. They all describe you as hard-working, honest and compassionate — just the sort of person we'd want in the United States."

"Thank you," said Papa.

"However," continued the consul, "I am missing a critical document — an affidavit from someone in the United States saying they would sponsor you or provide financial support for you. You do have this wonderful friend, with an unpronounceable name, who lives in Brazil. It's remarkable — you went to grade school together, to high school together, to college together. You both left Hungary about the same time and went to Vienna and played chamber music together. You married about the same time and your first children were born about the same time. That's a remarkable friendship and it tells me a lot about you."

The consul was speaking of Willy Rózsavölgyi, who had been Papa's friend in the early days in Vienna. He had immigrated to Brazil before we arrived and now lived with his family in São Paulo.

"Now," the consul continued, "your friend wants to help you

by making available to you some money that he has in the United States. It's not quite enough but it's a good beginning."

"I am sorry," said Papa, "but I cannot really take that money. Willy needs it for his business. He exports Brazilian goods to America and imports American goods here. The money he's offering is really his working capital."

"Well, I can see that you are a decent and kind man but you are not helping me to help you," the consul said. "Is there someone who could sponsor you in the United States?"

Papa answered, "A former professor of mine from medical school lives in Cleveland, Ohio. He has written to say that he and his wife would be happy to take my family in until we are settled. Unfortunately," Papa continued, "Ohio has very stringent laws that would not give credit for my Viennese medical degree. I'd have to start medical school all over again. That's just not feasible."

Outside the office, an agitated Mutti couldn't sit still. The secretary answered a phone call. As she focused on that, Mutti decided to seize the opportunity. She walked briskly into the consul's office. "Excuse me for bursting in," said Mutti. "I am very upset. I think I've spoiled everything."

Papa introduced her and asked for an explanation.

"I went to the German Embassy. At first they were very friendly and helpful but then they discovered that you had been designated a Jew. They insisted that you change your name to Isador or Israel, which is a requirement for Jews in Germany. I got really angry and told them we weren't in Germany anymore and they could forget their anti-Jewish nonsense and I left. I hope my outburst hasn't spoiled everything."

The consul exclaimed, "That's an outrage. We'll teach those guys a lesson. We're going to get you into the United States even if I have to give the necessary affidavit of support myself. Come back tomorrow."

A few weeks later, we stood on the deck of a small cargo vessel destined for New York City in the United States.

I never learned how we received permission without a sponsor. The family lore is that the consul personally provided the letter of guarantee required for entry. In the 1980s, while George Shultz was Secretary of State, I filed a Freedom of Information Act request to examine the file on our admission to the U.S. There was no letter from the consul in the file. One has to infer that the consul simply waived the requirement for a U.S.-based guarantor.

A number of friends came to say good-bye. Two actually came on board the cargo ship. Kolszinski shook Papa's hand and said, "I wanted tell you how grateful I am for all you did for everyone in Barra. You did everything we asked and more and I know how the villagers respected the medical work you did for them. I hope all goes well for you in the United States."

Dr. Campos, in addition to bidding us farewell, told a ship officer that he knew, "Dr. Weiser is my best friend." That may have been an exaggeration, but it got a wonderful result: We were promoted to a better cabin.

On the dock, we could see some of the Jewish refugees we had met when we first arrived in Rio, some of the tenants of our boarding house and Tiburcio, Vargas and Fritz. We waved good-bye to them and to Brazil as the ship slipped away from the dock and headed out to sea.

These passport photos brought Mutti, Lisl and Hansi to the U. S. in 1941.

The journey to New York City took several weeks as our small ship made stops at a number of ports to load and unload cargo. We stopped at a city at the mouth of the Amazon River; the ocean had a muddy color for miles before we reached shore. We had time to go ashore and went to the local zoo. I particularly remember a tank containing a large eel, which I was told was electric and would give you a dangerous shock if you touched it. That was scary.

The ship also stopped in Caracas, Venezuela. Here we were not allowed to disembark. The local authorities seemed to fear that this family with German passports might be spies.

Mutti used the time on board to start to teach English to Lisl and me. It seemed a remarkable language. I remember being surprised by the difference between the spelling and the pronunciation of words. Like the word "people": Americans pronounced it as though it was phonetically spelled "peepel," but Brazilians, giving phonetic weight to each letter, would pronounce it "pay-oh-play." The winner was the name of a famous writer, Shakespeare. Portuguese pronunciation would make it "shah-kay-spi-ah-ray."

And then the day came when we sailed into New York harbor. We all stood on the deck along the railing watching the tall buildings of the city come closer to us. But our eyes were drawn to the Statue of Liberty. We had seen pictures of it but now it was there in front of us. I thought it looked impressive but for Papa and Mutti it must have had a much deeper meaning. They stood side by side, arms around each other's backs, with Lisl and me leaning into them on either side. They didn't say anything but I could sense that they felt a deep gratitude.

Mutti later said that as we sailed by the Statue of Liberty, Papa stopped worrying. He knew there was a lot of work ahead but he believed very strongly that with hard work everything was now possible.

I hoped we'd finally find a home.

Epilogue

For the Weiser family, arrival in the United States was entering the Promised Land. The story in the United States was a long and happy one. Still, there were some difficult times in the early days, before things righted themselves.

On our arrival, the Committee for Catholic Refugees from Germany, an affiliate of the Catholic Church located in New York City, found us a fifth-floor walk-up studio apartment on the west side of New York City. Papa passed the examination for doctors to be licensed to practice medicine and then had to go through the normal internship and residency. He was happy to do that but the pay was meager. So Papa and Mutti made the difficult decision to send me to a boarding school in upstate New York, a seven-hour train ride from New York City. The Christian Brothers who operated the school accepted me at no cost to the family. I lived and studied there for two years before Papa was able to open an office, begin his own practice and earn enough money to bring me home. It was particularly important to Mutti to have me back; she had been deeply distressed when she came into the room and I stood up as I had been trained to do when an adult entered. Her distress deepened when she made a request and I responded with an innocent but distant "yes, ma'am." I had almost become a stranger.

Once Papa had some income, he and Mutti regularly sent CARE packages to their families in Europe. One package to Vienna included peanut butter and marshmallows. Years later my cousin, Hans Huber, told me that on receipt of that package, he concluded that we lived in a children's paradise. Mutti was a prodigious letter-writer and regularly corresponded with family and friends in Europe. Shortly after World War II ended, she went to Vienna to visit Omama (Opapa had died during the war) and her siblings.

Papa made one trip to Budapest to visit his sister and her family. Grandma Paula's story is tragic. She went into hiding near the war's end when the Nazis took control of Hungary and began a campaign of rounding up Jews to send to camps. Her hiding place was discovered and as Nazis came to take her, she took an overdose of her medicine, taking her own life.

Papa and Mutti regularly held chamber music sessions at their apartment. Both of them also actively participated in the Center Symphony Orchestra, an amateur group in Manhattan. Mutti took up the cello when she was 60 years old because it was often difficult to find cellists for their chamber music groups. She continued to play it into her late 80s.

In New York, Papa's office was in their apartment on the east side of Manhattan. He died of cancer in 1975, in a hospital near their apartment, at the age of 76. Mutti lived in that apartment for almost fifty years, until I brought her to an assisted living facility near me in the San Francisco Bay Area. She died there in 1995, aged 91.

Her grandchildren were the main beneficiaries of her imagination and creativity. They still relish memories of the suspenseful tension they felt as Mutti captured them with yet another night-time story full of suspense and excitement.

In the U.S. I was known as John. I graduated from Harvard Law School, then joined and eventually became a partner at Shearman and Sterling, a major Wall Street law firm. After twenty years there, I succeeded Caspar Weinberger as general counsel of Bechtel Corp., a global engineering-construction firm. After I retired from

Bechtel, I served as chair of the board of the Graduate Theological Union, an interfaith and interdenominational partnership of nine seminaries in the San Francisco Bay Area. Later, I was chair of the President's Council of the United Religions Initiative, the largest global interfaith network in the world.

I married Maria Cirigliano on February 20, 1954. We had nine children, one of whom died as a toddler, and as of this writing, we have eleven grandchildren. Our offspring live all over the U.S. Seven of our grandchildren have finished college and are working in the New York area or on the West Coast; three of them are attending colleges in Canada, Colorado and South Carolina, and the youngest is in grammar school in the New York area.

Lisl, who came to be known as Elizabeth in the U.S., has also had a satisfying and productive life. After graduating from Man-

Theresa, Arthur and Elizabeth celebrate John and Maria's wedding in New York City on February 20, 1954, honoring a new beginning for the Weiser family.

hattanville College in Westchester, N.Y., she worked at Standard Oil of New Jersey, with a small team that directly served the board of directors. In New York she met Dimitri Papadimitriou. Dimi had graduated from Bates College and was serving in the U.S. Army stationed in New Jersey. They married and lived for a time in New York, where Dimi became an officer of Chase Manhattan Bank. They moved to Europe, where he had lived as a child. He spoke several languages and eventually headed several of Chase's major offices in Europe. Lisl did an excellent job hosting visiting dignitaries including Chase Bank president David Rockefeller. She and Dimi had two sons and eventually, on Dimi's retirement, moved to Geneva, Switzerland, where she continued to live after Dimi's death.

Fortunately, the household goods my parents had stored in Vienna survived the war and they were able to bring to their New York apartment the grand piano and several works of art. Neither Papa nor Mutti showed any great interest in returning to Europe or making further visits. They had now made their life in the United States. Perhaps their attitude was colored by unhappy memories of the many ordinary Viennese who abetted brutal acts of the Nazis and by being disowned in their last months in Vienna by acquaintances and former friends.

On the other hand, as adults, Lisl and I were interested in reestablishing ties with family members in Europe and worked hard to maintain successful ties with cousins in Vienna and Budapest. We have made frequent visits and Maria and I hosted cousins and their children visiting the United States. Lisl, living in Europe, is in regular touch with her cousins there. In particular, one of her grandnieces studying in Geneva pays regular visits to her.

We discovered that the Metzger cousins included a number of very successful individuals: the founder of the Green Cross, an educational and lobbying group for medical patients; a successful industrial chemist who headed the Austrian Chemical Society; a distinguished professor of medicine; the founder and head of an international property appraisal firm; two leading journalists; the creator of the first Internet bank; the founder and head of Austria's first hospital management company; and a prizewinning organist.

As for our Brazil connections, the Burjans moved to New York after the war and we visited them in their apartment on Central Park West overlooking Central Park. The baron stayed where he was. For my eightieth birthday, my oldest son, John, took me back to Brazil and to Barra. There is now a well-paved road from Campos to Barra; the paving stops at the outskirts of the town, which still has dirt streets. We located the baron's house, preserved as a local monument, but there were only skeletal remains of the tapioca plant. We also found a Brazilian website that recounted that Baron Ludwig Kummer had built a second, larger tapioca plant a few miles upriver from Barra. The website further suggested that the baron's business had fallen on hard times when the law requiring use of tapioca in flour was repealed after the war. It also said that following the war the baron was investigated for possibly being a Nazi sympathizer. It does not appear that any charges were brought.